PRAISE FOR *SOMEDAY IS TODAY*

"Few books tackle the challenges of our times in ways that are real, compassionate, and impactful. *Someday is Today* does exactly that and thoughtfully brings the perspectives and voices that are most silenced from the dominant narrative to the forefront in a way that is engaging and full of depth. Readers gain rich insight into the complex issues that lie ahead and also receive practical solutions for having conversations at the individual and organizational levels. This book is a must-read for leaders looking for the truth of how to make change within themselves and within their teams and organizations."

—DR. ERIKA POWELL

"Allison Manswell has written an important book to remind us that the strides we make in DE&I call for urgency, and we cannot conveniently fall back on stating that it is a 'journey'. In *Someday is Today*, she is unflinching about the truth of where we are, the barriers still faced, and the bigotry and power struggles that continue. Manswell uses a story and dialogue format very effectively and the analogies and examples her characters use make the issues very relatable; and the ideas and checklists they provide are actionable.

Someday is Today has important nuggets for any business leader who wants to succeed and make an impact in today's world and importantly, to build for the future."

—DR. SARASWATHY (SARA) NOCHUR

SOMEDAY IS TODAY

SOMEDAY IS TODAY

ACHIEVING RACIAL EQUITY
IN THE WORKPLACE

ALLISON MANSWELL

Advantage | Books

Published by Advantage, Charleston, South Carolina.
Member of Advantage Media.

ADVANTAGE is a registered trademark, and the Advantage colophon is a trademark of Advantage Media Group, Inc.

Printed in the United States of America.

10 9 8 7 6 5 4 3 2 1

ISBN: 978-1-64225-967-4 (Hardcover)
ISBN: 978-1-64225-966-7 (eBook)

Library of Congress Control Number: 2024905423

Cover and layout design by Lance Buckley.

This publication is designed to provide accurate and authoritative information in regard to the subject matter covered. It is sold with the understanding that the publisher is not engaged in rendering legal, accounting, or other professional services. If legal advice or other expert assistance is required, the services of a competent professional person should be sought.

To my sons, family members, and friends, thank you for the love that gives me the courage to speak my piece.

To my PFC team whose commitment to our mission and our clients yields the most amazing results, thank you.

To George Floyd and those before him whose sacrifice went unnoticed, thank you.

To those soldiers and allies who refuse to be silenced, thank you.

CONTENTS

FOREWORD
BY TERRENCE FLOYD

Never in the history of the world have we seen streets flooded with protestors, on every continent, like we did the day after my brother, George Floyd Jr., was murdered. The unified cry for justice from those millions of people, showed that no race, gender, or creed has been exempted from the broken systems that were supposed to be in place to protect us. Since that day, my work has been to be a lighthouse, illuminating the direction of the path so the statements on our raised banners never go silent.

I have now found myself in many spaces around the world, partnering with individuals and organizations to create change for a better tomorrow for all of mankind. Looking for concrete solutions with proper actions, it became very noisy hearing so many people just speaking out. That is why I was profoundly drawn to the title of Allison's book, *Listen In*. In this book, Allison led us from the imperceptible to the practical with designs and tactics to support her philosophical statements such as "We will never make progress on Wall Street unless we get people to care about our lives on Main Street." After explaining how to do this work, she is now leading us into when to do this work with the sequel, *Someday is Today*.

This book is the holistic solution set we desperately need to ensure that equity is embraced and executed by employers. Organizations cannot have integrity about corporate social responsibility while upholding policies, procedures, and people who perpetuate a culture where only the majority succeed. *Listen In* and *Someday is Today* explore these answers and are a great place for committed leaders to gain strategies that can be implemented with a balanced approach.

It was important for me to know that Allison's commitment to equity began long before the summer of 2020. Her education and professional expertise make her a logical authority in this space and an ideal leader for the next phase of the movement.

The injustices in this world, like the one my brother endured, are not in vain when we "Listen in!" In the words of the great songwriter, "we shall overcome, someday". And in the words of Allison Manswell, "Someday is Today!"

INTRODUCTION

This book was incredibly hard to write. Maybe because I have taken on such a daunting task, but mostly because it challenged my faith in humanity.

I am a steward of the download. My first book on this topic, *Listen In: Crucial Conversations on Race in the Workplace*, felt like it was a divine gift. For eight years, people were asking me when the sequel to *Listen In* was coming out. The problem is that I am not a traditional author who sits down to write a book for personal satisfaction, public validation, or even financial gain. I always knew that when the characters were ready to resume this story—it would become distractingly obvious.

On March 10, 2022, my team and I participated in the Walk for Harriet Tubman, a commemoration of the 200th anniversary of her birth sponsored by GirlTrek.org. I started off by explaining my unique connection to Miss Harriet and Madame CJ Walker. They are the ancestors I have chosen to walk with me on my life's journey. It is also possible that I have been chosen to be an embodiment of their life's mission.

This made perfect sense to all of us at work since our work feels like the Underground Railroad 2.0. My education, experience, and unique combination of skills qualify me to use organizational effectiveness, talent management, and leadership development best practices as the path forward to racial equity in the workplace. In service of that mission, I have recruited a network of brilliant and committed people who pour their hearts and souls into this endeavor.

That day, I got a new connotation of the path forward that never occurred to me before: the path we clear publicly for leaders and organizations to follow. And then there is what feels like an underground railroad of survival tips and strategic maneuvers that someone needs to whisper in Black people's ears to help them navigate through this experience in the corporate wilderness. My role feels like an essential combination of how cornrows gave us a map and how Madame CJ's example orients us toward reclaiming wealth. Ironically, I have also had to come to terms with being in the initial stages of hearing loss since I wrote *Listen In*. Clearly God has jokes for my life. The moment the doctor turned my hearing aids on lives as the simulated Aha moment that I am always striving to create for others. That moment when something sounds altered, clearer and lands in your spirit differently than it ever has before. Listen for those moments while you read, or listen to this book and resist the urge to think that what you were experiencing before is 100 percent of the understanding available to you.

This also amplifies the point we have been hearing so clearly since the pandemic—be kind to people. You have no idea what they may be going through. It might be the visible effects of a diversity element that you can see (like race), or it may be an invisible challenge that they suffer with silently. I have reluctantly accepted that empathy does not come naturally to everybody. So, for some people, the best coaching I could offer is—be the person your dog thinks you are.

My writing process was going well. And then I hit a wall. At first, I thought it was me; maybe my creative juices just dried up or my brain was clogged with my CEO responsibilities. It was becoming clear that the critical mass of allyship and outpouring of commitment to racial equity was drying up and being replaced with empathy fatigue. It took me months to figure out that phenomenon was sucking up the optimism I required to finish this book. I struggled with the reality that many in the demographic who just "woke up" in 2020 were already denouncing being woken and using the term to be public about their intention to hit the snooze button.

Besides that paralyzing disappointment, it took me a long time to figure out why this book did not feel finished. Although it is a sequel, the vibe is different from *Listen In* where the focus was on promoting awareness through the characters. In this book, the focus is on motivating through solutions. My focus eventually returned. And after a period that once again felt divinely inspired, the characters pushed me over the finish line with their bare hands.

As usual with me, this book is not for everyone. I am not in pursuit of likes nor do I need approval from the masses. This book asks tough questions to get a polarized nation to consider both sides. If the notion of racial equity does not resonate with you—keep scrolling. However, if this outcome, these characters, their stories, the business consulting solutions, its depth, and potential as a catalyst for sustainable progress moves you—please stay in touch and let us know the impact it creates in your life. That is my highest intention.

1

WE SHALL OVERCOME

REWIND

The last time they had seen each other in person was right before the pandemic. Travelling in to reconnect at their favorite restaurant in DC without the worry of masks or social distancing added to the excitement of the reunion.

So much had happened since the last time they were all in person. LaToya and Shane left and were now living in Los Angeles. Roshunda made a career switch to HR after figuring out that she wanted to be part of the changes that needed to be made. After Eli's big reveal about being gay, he and Nathan had started spending more time with the group as a couple. Maya was still out in the world as an entrepreneur doing her own thing.

The Happy Hour Posse was seated at their favorite roundtable, just beside the bar. Everyone hung on her every word as LaToya began to spill the latest tea from her job.

"I leaned in, picked up my handbag, and left," LaToya said locking eyes with everyone to punctuate the seriousness of her statement.

"That's it? You left?" Eli asked. He sounded shocked at the anti-climactic nature of this ending.

"Yeah, I grabbed my pocketbook and sashayed my Black ass out of the conference room. I had had enough. What you're not going to do is insult me in a forum of my peers and direct reports," LaToya said. She stuck her fork into her appetizer as she continued speaking. The way she grabbed the handle, everyone could tell that LaToya was not over the incident. "We aren't going to write this off as a microaggression, and come back with a, 'He didn't mean any harm' bullshit response. In that moment, my silence and my absence was my statement." LaToya carefully placed a bite in her mouth, chewed methodically, and leaned back in her seat, giving everyone time to digest what she had just said.

Everyone looked at each other as if the initial fog of the moment had cleared up. That response made perfect sense for who they all knew LaToya to be. She could be the calm before the storm, or she could be the storm. Everyone had the ability to choose which version of her they experienced.

LaToya took their silence as permission to continue. "Listen, I have survived a global pandemic, buried loved ones by Zoom, managed depression and grief while in quarantine, been forced to relive images of George Floyd being tortured for over nine minutes, cry out for his Mama, and then take his last breath for the world to see. I refuse to tolerate any more injustice in the streets or racial inequity at work. Someday is today." LaToya grabbed her wine glass, raising it up for a toast. Others followed suit, each raising their glasses awaiting her final statement. "I know that I am not the only one that this has ever happened to. Black people need to decide to handle issues around race differently." she concluded.

"I will drink to that," Eli said. Everyone's glasses clinked in agreement.

LaToya felt validated to see that everyone understood her risky decision in that moment. However, she still couldn't stop replaying the scenario and wondering what was said after her grand exit. She expected a meeting invite from Susan to follow shortly. In a weird coincidence that felt like an alternate universe, Susan had a similar experience in a meeting that day.

———————

Susan drove home with an anxious grip on the steering wheel. She was still processing what happened and couldn't wait to share the story with Jim. She found him in his office staring blankly at the screen. He looked overwhelmed and lost. She remembered the tactic she learned in marriage counseling and decided it would be best to wait patiently until after dinner to bring up her work issues.

When she couldn't keep her peace any longer, Susan began, "You are not going to believe what happened in the senior leadership meeting today. We had a full house in the room and two vendors on Zoom. Granted, the comment made was inappropriate. Sven tried to make a joke by comparing the number of changes being made to the strategy to the amount of changes Fatima makes to her hairstyles. He didn't mean it to be offensive. We all know he says dumb stuff like that all the time." Susan paused for a moment, making sure Jim was able to follow along.

"He has made lots of comments about women, the LGBTQIA+ community, and everyone. But Fatima's response was a little extreme— she just left. No explanation. No nothing. I was so embarrassed. Everyone looked at me as if I knew why. We waited for a moment, but she never came back. Eventually we just picked up the conversation and moved on. It was incredibly awkward." Susan waited for an expression of empathy to match her shock.

Jim took his napkin and wiped the corners of his mouth. He looked at her and reluctantly asked, "What did you say?" In his heart he knew the answer, but still hoped she would surprise him with a teachable moment one would expect from the Chief HR Officer.

Susan pushed her food around on her plate before responding. She could feel the discomfort setting in between her and her husband. She let out a deep sigh, taking her time to be cautious about how she responded. "I didn't know what to say. All I could think about was how everyone at the table was feeling, and how this response damaged her credibility as the only woman of color on the senior leadership team." Susan stopped to study Jim's response across the dinner table. Although he was attentive, he seemed to be choosing his words carefully. She struggled to discern if he agreed or disagreed with her.

Jim allowed himself to feel through this powerful moment where he hung in the balance between deep love for his life partner and frustration over the level of fragility that she continued to demonstrate. He finally brought himself to launch a strategic conversation summary he hoped would lend itself to a more robust conversation another day.

"Honestly, Susan, I get it. I feel like she left because it was the safest and most professional response she could muster at that moment. I don't think any of you could have handled the full explanation that you probably deserved. Specifically, how offensive the analogy about her hair was, how many times she has probably let comments slide, the polite responses, and subtle education she has already provided," Jim added. Susan's eyes widened as she tried to process his take on this.

"I have been actively working on racial equity in my company for several years. One thing that is clear to me now is that at some point, we as white people are going to have to realize that we have entered a new era. No one is putting up with microaggressions at work anymore. No one wants to hear about the diversity, equity, and inclusion (DEI) 'journey.' That approach is a stall tactic for a trip we don't want to take. The days of 'we shall overcome' are over. Someday is today."

2

WE ARE
NOT ALONE
GENERATIONAL DIFFERENCES

Roshunda was nervous. The thought of asking Maya to serve as a mentor to a group of young professionals seemed like a setup for the sarcastic responses she was known for. After about fourteen email drafts describing the group Roshunda had assembled and her request for Maya as a mentor, she realized this request would be better received face-to-face.

She decided to invite Maya out for coffee, hoping a casual meet up would help her request land more sincere. Roshunda was already seated at a corner table when Maya arrived and she flagged her over. After they exchanged greetings, and she let Maya give the long version of an update on her children, Roshunda jumped right in.

"Maya, I know we have not always seen eye to eye. But I hope you know how much I respect you, your wisdom, and all that you have accomplished in your life. Besides your successful transition out of corporate America, I admire the way you coach and mentor the young people in your life. You just have that cool Auntie vibe that makes young people gravitate toward you. I wondered if you would be open to serving as a mentor for a group of young professionals that I have assembled?" Roshunda paused, allowing her question to land.

Maya rolled her eyes and paused for a moment. "Thank you for the compliment. I have grown up with a mix of all generations around me. As a child, I was raised in a household with teenagers, adults, and elders. And I never realized how much that impacted my outlook. But I must admit that a mentoring assignment sounds challenging for me. You young people think you know every damn thing. Why would I sign up for that frustrating assignment? Y'all don't listen and what's worse, your ignorance is exasperated by impatience. I love the idea of mentoring, but I find your generational arrogance challenging." Maya took a sip from her steaming mug and appeared to be waiting for additional justification to validate the request.

Roshunda needed a minute to process the honesty of Maya's response. She expected Maya to be resistant, but she didn't want to give up so soon. "What we really need are frank conversations like this between the different generations. If I promise to establish a safe space for their listening, would you be willing to do just one session?"

Maya didn't need much time to craft her reply. She truthfully had a lot of respect for millennials, their tenacity, courage, and ability to leverage technology. Without letting Roshunda know how excited she was for the opportunity and how honored she was to be asked, she simply replied, "OK, fine. I will try it because I know there is a lot I can learn from them as well."

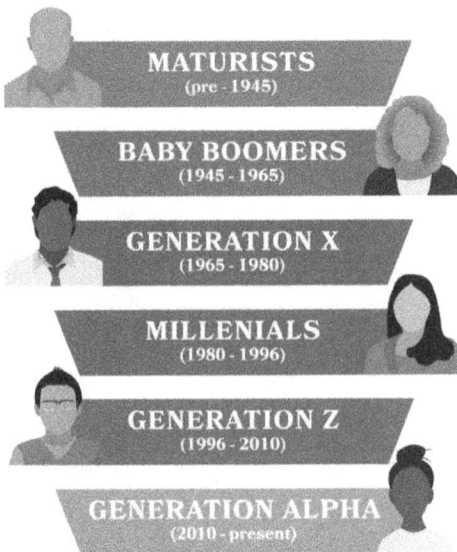

MATURISTS
(pre - 1945)

BABY BOOMERS
(1945 - 1965)

GENERATION X
(1965 - 1980)

MILLENIALS
(1980 - 1996)

GENERATION Z
(1996 - 2010)

GENERATION ALPHA
(2010 - present)

Truthfully, Roshunda was covertly using this group mentoring assignment as a front to get private time with Maya for coaching of her own. She appealed to her ego by asking, "Maybe you can give me some advice on something that I am currently going through."

Maya gave Roshunda the side eye. "Sure, what's going on?" she answered without missing a beat.

Roshunda placed her cup on the table and straightened her posture. "I recently made a post on LinkedIn that was well thought through, admittedly a little edgy, and I am struggling with some of the backlash I have received. I commented on yet another McKinsey and Lean In study on how Black women leaders are more ambitious and less supported than others. My caption was: How many more studies must we endure before anything changes? I am beginning to wonder if a nation-wide strike by Black women could be a potential path forward."

Roshunda took a moment to gather her thoughts before she continued. It was in this moment she realized truly how affected she was by this. "I am so disappointed by the comments I heard from white people I respected, and Black people I thought were woke. They jumped in with the struggle Olympics about how other groups experience a lack of support as well. It all sounded like a deflection of the core issue at hand."

Maya sat with a "bless your heart" look on her face. "That is a good place to start this generational conversation. Millennials have made social media far too important in their world. Because it has been such an integral part of your life and given you way more power than you earned or were ready for, you allow it to take on more meaning than it should. Social media is the only therapy some people have. When you realize what that means it will change how you engage online and the weight you give to people's comments," Maya took a sip of her cappuccino. "Your responsibility is to follow each platform's guidelines, think through your posts, and consider current and future impact. If you decide that a controversial thought is worth sharing, then get out your feelings when people disagree because that's what you signed up for when you put your thoughts out there. That's why I don't even post that much on any platform. I don't care that much about what other people think about my ideas."

Maya's comment hit Roshunda hard and she realized why they say that people in different generations have different perspectives. Until that moment, it never really dawned on her what a world could look like without social media or technology. "What was life like before social media?" Roshunda asked, with genuine curiosity laced in her question.

"It could be important for more millennials and younger ones to understand that there was a world before social media," Maya responded. "We used to communicate first by letter, then by telephone, and we relied a lot more on face-to-face interaction. Now I will admit, it didn't give us the kind of reach that you guys have." Maya could tell Roshunda was pleased to hear her give millennials and younger people some credit. She didn't want to discourage her and knew that she needed to highlight some positives from this generation. "So, one of the things I admire about your generation is the sheer volume of people that you have access to. I personally believe that's part of why you are all better at DEI than we are. Because you've had access to so many more people, you've seen so many different versions of what awesome looks like. In addition, you have an action item to hit 'like' when you get exposed to different people and ideas. The act of pressing like and endorsing other people's behaviors means that you are accustomed to seeing other people be great. And unfortunately, baby boomers and the silent/traditionalist generation didn't have the benefit of that."

Roshunda rested her chin on her fist and leaned in as she listened to Maya. Fascinated by this generational perspective, she had practically forgotten about the latte that was sitting in front of her. "On the one hand, you guys are farther ahead than we were when it comes to worldliness at a young age. But on the other hand, y'all have the false confidence that information equals wisdom. That's why we call you the '*dummies with the smart phones.*'"

They both broke out laughing knowing that it was an inappropriate generalization that was grounded in truth. When Roshunda got herself together, she asked, "Wait, why do they call them baby boomers?"

Maya rolled her eyes and looked to the heavens to get an answer. "It's the name given to the older generation that is about as old as your parents right now. They're called baby boomers because they were born after World War II when soldiers came back from the war. Because they were so *happy* to see their significant others, there was a *boom* of babies." Maya shook her head in disbelief over Roshunda not knowing what the very common term meant. "That's a real gap in today's educational system; the fact that you all are not learning some tangible aspects of generational differences. So let me back up for a moment and give you some definitions," Maya said while placing her mug back down.

Roshunda asked, "What do you think are some of the key differences in generations that we need to know?"

Maya paused, and then started. "Well, what I just mentioned is probably the first one. The volume of people that social media gave you access to, and the way it has expanded your view of the world is probably the number one difference between the generations. And I think it's a real benefit for your generation. Second, we, meaning us Gen Xers, over-parented you guys. That's how we got to be called the helicopter generation because we hovered around your every move and made sure that you were involved in every single extracurricular activity. We made a valiant attempt to be more involved than our parents were in our lives."

"The output of that is that we gave you first, second, and third place trophies for winners and a participation ribbon for everyone else. And although at first glance we thought it was the right thing to do because it helped everybody feel included, that phenomenon had a couple of downsides. First of all, it gave you the false impression that you will be rewarded just for effort and not your results. Second of all, it made you obsessed with getting positive feedback, and in some cases unable to accept criticism; and it gave you the idea that the world is fair. And that last one is a double-edged sword because unfortunately, the world is not fair. The world is not gonna treat you fair if you are white, and it's certainly not gonna treat you fair in your Black body. However, what those participation ribbons also gave many white people is a commitment to equity that could become a force to be reckoned with in the workplace. Because you have this innate idea that everyone should be treated the same, you actually have a better chance than any generation of making real progress towards equity." Maya realized she had just said a mouthful and could see Roshunda processing the information. "Does that make sense?"

Roshunda nodded slowly while taking another big sip. A lot of what Maya said made perfect sense. And then, there was a lot that she didn't completely agree with. She wanted to wait until Maya completed her thoughts before offering her own opinion.

"Now, I'd like to ask you the same question. What do you think the older generations need to know about you and your peers?" Maya asked.

Roshunda paused for a while. She wanted to make sure she was as thoughtful as Maya had been. She started off by saying, "I acknowledge that the younger generation has not always respected the wisdom of the elders. We are out here pretending we know everything because of what technology has given us. And we own that. I also think that every generation thinks they are the *best* generation. I'm sure when everyone was smoking weed and having sex at Woodstock, their parents were mortified and thought those people wouldn't amount to anything. In addition, I also think that the older generation does not give us enough credit for the impact of what we know, our work ethic, or the fact that things don't have to be done like in the old days. It is OK to change and evolve."

"Tell me more," Maya said warmly.

"For example," Roshunda started, "I hear a lot of technology bashing without acknowledgment that processes are improved, productivity is increased, and money is saved when we leverage technology. It is not all bad and some of the outcomes are pretty awesome. For example, ChatGPT will soon replace standard Google searches and we can't even fathom the impact of what that means," Roshunda said, her excitement at the idea showing itself in her hand gestures.

Maya smiled, nodded, and glossed over the fact that she had no idea what ChatGPT was.

"I hear all the time that our generation is lazy," Roshunda continued. "And we don't want to work as hard as everyone else. And I really resent that because it's not true. What I see from me, and my friends, is that we work just as hard, if not harder, than our older peers. We're just committed to working smarter. We sign on after work, we stay up late and make sure we get our deliverables done. But what we're not gonna do is waste a bunch of time standing at the Keurig machine, and then come home to do a bunch of busy work in our discretionary time. I think we are more apt to use technology in ways that are more efficient, but that doesn't make us lazy." Roshunda paused to give Maya a chance to respond.

"Touché. That is correct. We do assume that you all don't work as hard as us. And that you stay chillin' with ear buds in your ears," Maya said.

"And that's another thing," Roshunda added, pointing a finger in the air to note the point she was about to make. "Having music playing in our ears doesn't mean that we are 'chillin.' Many of us grew up with multiple devices on in the background. So now, we are programmed to think in stereo. Also, the speed of the TV programming we watch is much faster than what you guys watched. So, we take in information at a faster speed. Sometimes it's cognitively hard to interact with others who process so slowly."

Maya didn't know how she felt about being accused of processing slowly, but she understood how and why the younger generation had an innate need for multiple forms of stimulation.

Roshunda interrupted Maya's thoughts to continue. "Just because we don't want to stay at work and make time and a half pay, doesn't mean we don't have a small business at home that will pay us triple or quadruple what overtime would net. It also doesn't mean that in addition to our jobs, we're not participating in the gig economy by driving for Lyft, DoorDash or Airbnbing out our house when we go on vacation. Those are opportunities that were not available to the previous generations. And we don't get any credit for being smart enough to have invented them and having the wherewithal to use them."

Roshunda did a classic mirror and match technique where she copied Maya's body language and then asked, "Does that make sense?"

Maya had no choice but to admit, "Yes, it absolutely does. You are right."

Roshunda was surprised to hear Maya give her the long overdue recognition and credit for her generation. She paused briefly, taking in the small win before proceeding. "Another thing I believe is important for the older generation to know about us is that we don't appreciate you making us feel like your children in the workplace. We understand we're old enough to be your son or daughter, but when someone uses that language, they create an automatic power dynamic that is not empowering, and it doesn't feel good at all. So, part of the reason why we don't ask you for help is because you make us feel less than for having asked for your help. It would benefit us all if the older generation could put their ego aside and offer help to us as peers, as opposed to subordinates just because of our age."

"That's fair. I never thought of it that way," Maya said as she leaned back in her seat, clearly having a prolonged Aha moment that caught her off guard.

Roshunda was relieved to see Maya responding so well to the points she made. She was also surprised by how much of her own advice she had to offer on the topic. "The issues around DEI are another dividing line between generations. We simply don't understand what is taking you all so long to make progress on treating people fairly. As much as I believe we have it much better than previous generations, as a result we have blind spots on issues related to race. At some point, we are going to have to shed the victim mentality and start creating the new reality we want. If I hear 'we shall overcome someday' one more time, I'm gonna scream. Enough—someday is today." Roshunda took a gulp of her drink with that final thought.

Maya nodded her head in agreement. "Preach Sis. I am the choir, been saying this for years. It's refreshing to hear you voice it though. I can't wait for your generation to channel all of that allyship energy I saw after George Floyd's killing into a sustainable commitment to change. I hope we don't have to wait until all of you get into leadership roles in the workplace," Maya finished as she glanced down at her watch. She didn't realize how much time had passed during their conversation.

Roshunda continued as if she didn't notice Maya monitoring the time. "And the last thing that I think is important for the older generation to know about us is that we are morphing into different generations really fast. I know it's convenient to call us all millennials, but we're technically not all millennials. There's the oldest group of millennials; those are kind of like the OG millennials. The official word for them right now is the Bridgers, who are classified as those born between 1982 and 2002."

"They have children that are in elementary and middle school right now. Then come the Gen Zs who are between eleven and twenty-six years old. Gen Zs are also the little brothers and sisters of the millennials. They have a mildly different approach as well, because they have had cellphones all their lives. And then finally, we are now beginning to notice what they call Gen Alpha, who are the children impacted by COVID. Gen Alpha are the youngsters from toddler to elementary school age range who were either born or in their formative years during COVID-19. They will forever be impacted by how those early years were changed because of the pandemic."

Roshunda took a breath as she realized she gave a lot of information in that moment. When she allowed the information to hit the air between them, she continued, "So, what we need the older generation to know is that they need to broaden their view of what the next generation looks like, learn about us, and begin to prepare for all the different ways we will change the workforce."

"You're absolutely right. We need to build alliances across generational differences and stop lumping you all into one big group with a narrow series of stereotypes," Maya said humbly. "You sure learned me something today," she chuckled knowing that the phrase was a nod to her grandmother's generation. "I wish we could find a way to share this with more people."

Roshunda responded, "I think everybody needs a chance to have intergenerational conversations like this," smiling at Maya. "I'm so glad you agreed to be a mentor for us. I can't wait for the first session."

"Facts," Maya said, trying to sound cool. Roshunda looked at her with an endearing smile, acknowledging her sincere effort to demonstrate comradery.

Before heading out of the coffee shop, the two stood up from the table and exchanged a hug that felt like a reach between ancestors and future generations.

3

WE ARE
NOT AFRAID

RACE AND GENDER

Jasmine was head down nearly getting sucked into her computer while the Supreme Court of the United States confirmation hearings played on mute in the background. She was feeling an unsettling combination of annoyance and inspiration from Judge Ketanji Brown Jackson's confirmation process. She didn't have the time or emotional capacity to watch what felt like a public flogging of someone who could be her body double, but she wanted to witness history being made without having to hear the sound.

Her consulting practice was thriving and she was enjoying working with clients like Jim and his leadership team. He genuinely cared about the culture in his company and the DEI goals that were established long before George Floyd's killing. Her challenge was the stress of feeling like the clock was ticking on the 2020 empathy wave. She knew that if and when things went back to status quo—it would feel like the light had been turned off at the end of the tunnel.

However, in this moment she needed to dismiss all of that and become single-mindedly focused on reviewing the data from the most recent organizational assessment her firm was conducting, and she still needed to submit an outline to producers for her next show. She appreciated the recognition that came with her work but between client work and current events, she was feeling overwhelmed.

Jasmine wanted to run through the streets shouting for joy that Ahmaud Arbery's murderers were convicted. But somehow, even this verdict didn't ease the pain that Trayvon Martin's killer was still out living his best life. It felt like it had become an accepted part of American culture that the hunting and killing of Black people was the norm. At least now, in one state, legal precedence had been set and the monsters who perpetrated these crimes could be punished.

Jasmine rose from her living room couch and took a slow walk to the kitchen to pour a glass of wine. She returned in time to notice Senator Cory Booker at the microphone. She pushed her hand between the cushions to find her remote control and turned the volume up in time to hear Senator Booker's comments. His apology for his colleagues' behavior seemed completely appropriate given the embarrassing display of racism and absurdity. His expression of joy was exactly what sane people needed to hear; a coherent reminder that someone was listening to the embarrassing demonstration of due process on display. *We see you Judge Jackson. We hear you. We feel you.*

The groundswell of emotion she attempted to suppress during this process began to surface. Jasmine felt herself sitting in that chair on the Senate floor, absorbing the vile accusations and extreme disrespect in front of her colleagues, her husband, and her children. She wondered if she could have endured what Judge Jackson had to experience for ten minutes, much less five days. Without giving permission, her tears escaped. Jasmine sat back onto the sofa, and sobbed until the pain and promise of the moment left her body.

By the time the hearings were over and Judge Jackson was confirmed, Jasmine was ready to channel her thoughts and feelings into an appropriate LinkedIn post. Her fingers seemed to channel an energy of their own as she allowed herself to let every thought and every feeling transfer into the small, allotted space for her post. Version #84 of her caption would be shared with the *Washington Post* graphic that displayed her qualifications relative to all other justices.[1]

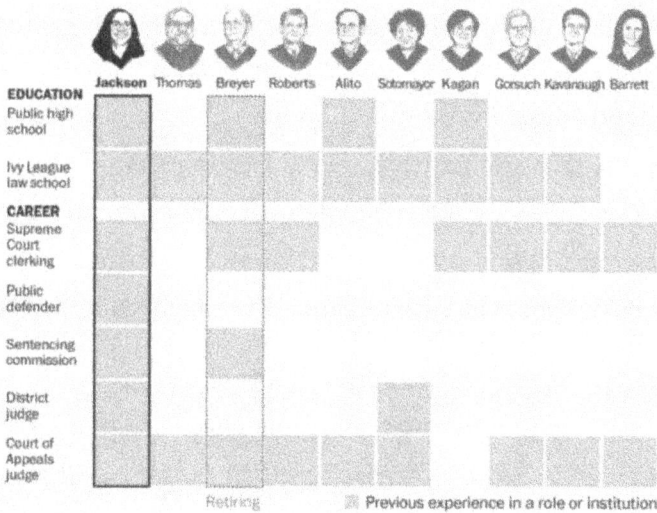

How Ketanji Brown Jackson's path to the Supreme Court differs from the current justices

	Jackson	Thomas	Breyer	Roberts	Alito	Sotomayor	Kagan	Gorsuch	Kavanaugh	Barrett

EDUCATION
Public high school

Ivy League law school

CAREER
Supreme Court clerking

Public defender

Sentencing commission

District judge

Court of Appeals judge

Retiring ▓ Previous experience in a role or institution

Congratulations to #JudgeKetanjiBrownJackson on your confirmation to #SCOTUS. So, the asinine questions you were asked and condescending tones will forever live as an example of the deliberate roadblocks that people of color experience on a regular basis in the workplace. This was a national display of us always having to work "twice as hard."

---

1 *The Washington Post*, How Ketanji Brown Jackson's path to the Supreme Court differs from the current justices, graphic, March 20, 2022.

Very often we deflect these realities by jumping into celebratory mode. Let us pause to admit that Judge Jackson should not have been made to endure this indignity. We don't need more accolades for our strength and #blackgirlmagic. We need people to stop putting us in situations where we have to demonstrate it. So, Judge Jackson, on behalf of those who notice the pain you endured so that your accomplishment could inspire us—we thank you. #KetanjiBrownJackson #SheWillRise

Jasmine gave her post one more read before hitting share, satisfied with every point she presented. She sat thinking about the magnitude of the indignities of this process. Neither political party put Judge Amy Coney Barrett or Judge Sonia Sotomayor through anything like this. Even white women joined in the foolishness. The irony of this abuse occurring during Women's History Month with such a lack of womanhood allyship was not lost on her.

Jasmine grabbed her wine, taking small sips as she continued to hear the live coverage and news updates of the hearings. Her thoughts were running a mile a minute, and the only way to get them out was to open a blank draft and begin typing her thoughts out as a blog post.

Besides the fact that Judge Jackson was being berated and bullied by a group of white men marginally qualified for their current roles, white women joined the chorus and did the same thing. All while knowing they were being televised, and that social media was adding the nation's commentary which they had probably read or been briefed on. This blatant display of bullying and disregard for the "women's movement" was a sad statement on the state of the relationship between Black and white women.

Jasmine was mid-thought when she realized that this was the topic for the next podcast: The "*Keisha and Karen Dialogues: Real*

Conversations on Race and Gender." Her next action item was to write an outline for producers and give suggestions for guests who might be willing to engage in a discussion about the reality of the relationship between Black and white women. Her fingers hit the keyboard like stilettos in a courtroom and she knew this episode would be lit.

TITLE: The Keisha and Karen Dialogues: Unpacking Race and Gender

TOPIC: The complicated relationship between Black and white women

FORMAT: Facilitated discussion with a mixed group of women

MODERATOR NOTES:

- We recognize these as the stereotypical names for Black and white women and I know that some people are triggered so let's address that first.

  - Keisha is a widely recognized ethnic name used to signal a previously unidentified Black woman.

    - The issue of ethnic names is a huge debate in the broader people of color community. Jose doesn't get called back until he changes his name to Joe. Adam gets called back for an interview 2.5 times more than Mohammed.

  - Karen is a label used to describe someone who wields and escalates her white privilege in no-risk situations sometimes as a weapon to inflict harm

- Both are being used here for ease of language and dramatic effect. Don't be in your feelings or in the comments whining if those are your actual names.

- I want to acknowledge that today's content contains triggering concepts that can potentially retraumatize groups impacted by this topic. While it is never my intention to contribute to this emotional distress, I recognize the value that these conversations offer in shifting perspectives and ultimately behavior. As usual, if your comments are disrespectful or deemed to be additionally hurtful, you will be disconnected and blocked.

- There is a complicated history between Black and white women that starts with slavery, continues through the Jim Crow era, and is perpetuated today.

  - Carolyn Bryant's role in lying and getting Emmett Till killed is perhaps the most widely reported case before Amy Cooper was recorded trying the same thing in Central Park.
  - From that moment on, we were all painfully advised that a white woman's story (true or false) can get Black people (specifically Black men) killed.
  - Carolyn Bryant just died and there was never any movement toward bringing her to justice for the original and legacy trauma of her lie. We lost an important opportunity to provide the reconciliation required to heal this wound.

- Here are a few questions to consider now:

  - What are the implications of this history?

- Are we willing to move through the discomfort to reconciliation?
- What needs to happen for this to occur?
- Is gender equality possible without this reconciliation?

- What do white women want to say to Black women?

- What do Black women want to say to white women?

- What generous assumptions can we give each other the benefit of?

- What role do Black men and white men play in this process?

- What are we missing about this relationship?

- I have heard it said that "White women participate in sexism so they can enjoy the benefits of racism."

- I have also heard it said that "Black women resent white women but find themselves having to adopt their characteristics in order to enjoy their benefits." Strong accusations. Let's debate.

- What do Black women need to know about how we contribute to and/or perpetuate this bad blood?

- What do white women need to know about how they contribute to and/or perpetuate this animosity?

- Where have we gotten this right? Positive examples.

- Where do we go from here?

Jasmine paused for a moment to reflect on the future impact of Carolyn Bryant's death. In that moment she found herself being sad for all the wrong reasons. Although she was alone, she felt the need to say her thoughts out loud. "I hope her soul never rests and she reaps the condemnation to hell that she deserves."

She sat back in her chair and looked at the screen. She imagined her listeners taking copious notes and using these questions to host roundtables and book club discussions. She knew this would be difficult for Black women to sit through and for white women to endure. But she also knew that this content would move the conversation forward to help both groups understand and hopefully resolve the issues between them.

4

WE SHALL
ALL BE FREE

SEXUAL ORIENTATION, GENDER
IDENTITY, AND EXPRESSION (SOGIE)

Nathan was still carefully selecting which social events to attend. He weighed the consequences of sharing aspects of his personal life with others as he enjoyed the benefits of being perceived as a straight Black man. Given his upbringing, the messages he received that connected his sexuality to his family's social status, he continued to decide situation by situation when to invite others in.

After spending time with each of Eli's friends one at a time, he felt much more comfortable being with all of them as a group. It was just a few weeks ago that Nathan and Eli met up with the whole gang for drinks. Everyone seemed genuinely friendly, and it turned out to be a great time. It also helped Nathan let his guard down a bit. Although they were all nice and never made him feel uncomfortable, there was just something about being invited to this conversation that felt like it was about to feel like an ERG panel discussion.

Roshunda originally asked Eli to have a conversation to help Maya understand more about the Lesbian, Gay, Bisexual, Transgender, and Queer (LGBTQ) experience. But Eli felt that Nathan would be a better choice because he was so much more comfortable than he was in a teaching conversation. Her and Maya's mentoring relationship was blossoming. But Maya needed insight on these issues as a follow-up to a conversation they had a few weeks ago. He appreciated the sincere and respectful way the invitation was issued, but still wondered if he would end up regretting it later. Until then, he committed himself to being appropriately delightful and as sarcastic as the moment called for.

Eli knew that a moment like this would eventually come. The transition from the joy and relief of coming out to his friends to now the anxiety of being an internal subject matter expert on being gay—was a lot to take in.

Roshunda was excited about this conversation and grateful that Nathan even agreed to share his knowledge. She understood the value of her and Maya gaining perspective and real information from him but was a little nervous about the process overall. From what she read on LinkedIn and inferred from Eli, Nathan was one of those W.E.B. Du Bois intellectual negroes with impressive degrees and over $100,000 in student loan debt. He had just gotten promoted before he finally went to his first corporate event with Eli. Other than that, he was a bit of a mystery to them. She hoped that he received the sincerity of her inquiry and that Maya wouldn't embarrass her with her blunt communication style.

As they sat down, the conversation flowed easily from one current event and related meme to the next. Roshunda had so many questions for Nathan. Her company had recently offered a course called "An Introduction to Sexual Orientation, Gender Identity and Expression (SOGIE)" and it was just as powerful as the course they offered on "Appreciating the Experience of Race at Work." One of the techniques taught by the company was known as the emotional preamble, which was a tool to introduce an awkward topic or question by acknowledging the discomfort surrounding it. She planned on practicing it this evening.

After it looked like everyone had finished their entrée, Roshunda slid right into the conversation. "Nathan, I really appreciate you joining us. As I mentioned in my invitation, I am hoping that you feel comfortable enough to give Maya and I some insight into your experience and your knowledge of SOGIE in general. I just learned that acronym. Is it OK if I ask you to share whatever you are comfortable with when you were coming out? What do we need to know?"

Everyone held their breath for a moment as they absorbed Roshunda's respectful introduction.

Nathan admired the care with which she posed the question and felt the sincerity of her ignorance. He replied, "First, let me make a disclaimer. I do not want to be the resident 'gay guy.' Secondly, sexuality and gender are both complex concepts that are often conflated to mean the same thing. What SOGIE represents is a way to express the diversity of a community of folks across a broad spectrum of sexualities, identities, and experiences. They are three separate topics in and of themselves. But I am happy to share my perspective as long as you receive it as just my perspective. I encourage you to engage in conversations like these with other people to get a more well-rounded understanding." Nathan leaned forward in his chair, resting his elbows on the table. "Gender identity and expression is about who you are and is very different from sexual orientation, which is about who you love. Because I am also cisgender, meaning that the way I identify in terms of my gender matches the sex I was assigned at birth, I am not the right person to speak for the trans community." Nathan realized that adding the definitions proactively would alleviate the awkwardness of them wondering and not feeling comfortable enough to ask for clarification.

He could tell by their squinting and eyebrow angles that they were encouraging him to continue. "We are all learning that language is continuously evolving. I'm even reconsidering my terms. Everyone, including me, has always said 'coming out' but now we realize that it's 'inviting others in.' That reframing allows for more agency and ownership. It's not about being reactive to others but being proactive about the choice to disclose. I invite people into knowing this part of myself when I feel that there is physical, emotional, and psychological safety to share." The group nodded reassuringly, confirming they were off to a good start.

Once Nathan let his guard down, he realized that Eli's friends were just a solid group of folks who happened to be cisgender, straight and their life experiences were just informed by their interactions primarily with other cis and straight individuals.

"I always wanted to be whole in the world someday," Nathan continued. "To be appreciated. To be loved—and to love. To be valued unconditionally. But I chose to put the value of my pedigree and my family's honor ahead of my need to live my truth. Coming from affluence meant there was the added burden of adhering to and upholding the harmful beliefs of the dominant white, heterosexual class. I ignored sexual orientation as a diversity element and allowed race to be my only limiting identifier. And I focused on the benefits from positive biases of education and socioeconomic class. I bought into those respectability politics for many years, until I couldn't do it anymore."

Nathan paused and allowed the weight of his commentary to linger for a moment before he continued. "Something shifted a few years ago that inspired my alignment. I finally started to listen in to the messages that my soul was sending me. My initial concern was about the scorn of Bible beating Christians who pretended to live their lives from scripture, until it came to eating shrimp and wearing clothes made from different fibers. I also let go of the hypocrisy of the Black Lives Matter folks who are totally comfortable telling gay jokes about Black people, while being clueless about the damage it inflicts. At least with racism we expect to not be accepted or included. Homophobia from your own people cuts a little deeper." Nathan raised his eyebrows and shrugged his shoulders as he took a sip of his drink.

Maya found herself moved by Nathan's experience. She realized that she was one of the people who carried deep-rooted ideas about sex and sexuality that probably brought pain to many people in her past. She said, "I must admit that I participated in a homophobic culture growing up. I was well into mature adulthood before I understood and began accepting an experience beyond a cisgender man and a cisgender woman together. Just when I felt like I understood the value of heterosexual privilege, along came the transgender and cisgender conversation and it threw me off a bit."

Nathan started by saying, "Congratulations on even being able to acknowledge that. Heterosexual privilege is like white privilege given to straight cisgender people. It's invisible and powerful. There are benefits to being in that majority; like putting up a picture of you and your significant other in a loving embrace without anyone accusing you of pushing your sex life in peoples' faces. Most people don't understand the embarrassment of having basic elements of your life sexualized," he added.

Nathan paused momentarily, anticipating the others having a follow-up comment on his experience. During the pause that followed, Nathan took a mental time-out to acknowledge what was occurring. He was in the precarious position of representing a community that has conflicts within itself on some of these topics. The fact that these were his partner's friends was only partial consolation for the emotional burden this role created. He understood that it would probably get worse before it got better because Maya had another question brewing on her face.

As if she had read his mind, Maya continued, "Nathan, I realize we are putting you in the same position that white people put us in. We hate it too. We are here asking you questions that you think we should already know. I feel so white right now," Maya chuckled. She hoped that adding a joke would help alleviate the discomfort of the dynamics. "Please know that my curiosity comes from a genuine desire to understand and do better. I must admit that I just do not know enough people that I have a relationship with to ask these questions. I don't want to bombard you tonight, but can we schedule another time to reconnect?" Maya asked.

As much as Nathan appreciated the respect of her approach, he had no desire to put himself back into this token gay man position again any time soon. "No, it's OK. I prefer to answer it here once than to risk my words getting lost in translation when you guys debrief this conversation without me." A touch of appropriate sarcasm was his only reprieve.

"Honestly," Maya began, "You should be teaching this somewhere. This opportunity to learn and understand is so important in alleviating the isolating behaviors that must be painful. I have a burning question that I have been wrestling with," Maya precautioned.

Nathan's jaw tightened as he braced himself to go further down the "teach me" rabbit hole.

"How did we get to the place of calling sex a social construct?" Maya asked. Nathan raised an eyebrow, to which Maya could tell she needed to better elaborate. "Follow me for a minute. It is the same confusion created when we say, 'race is a social construct.' People can see that there are physical, biological, and quantifiable differences between people from different regions of the world. Some people have more melanin in their skin than others. Sickle cell, which is an evolutionary adaptation to malaria exposure, impacts Black/African American people at a higher rate. Clinical trials need to be conducted on different human races to monitor variations in reactions across the different races. So, it is confusing for the average person (non-scientist) to understand why that is a 'social construct.'" Maya paused to collect her thoughts. "It looks like a biological fact. We would be better served to acknowledge that there are biological differences between people who originated from different regions of the world. From there, we can clarify that the social construct is that one group of people added a value judgment to these differences and said that Caucasian people are inherently superior. So, racial difference is not a social construct. The value judgment of white superiority is the social construct," Maya concluded.

Nathan paused before responding. He wanted to be very careful of his explanation. "I think you are interchanging the term sex with gender. Sex is biological. Gender is an expression of identity. That distinction is at the core of the point you are making," Nathan said. He knew Maya wasn't finished, so he waited patiently for her to formulate a coherent question that he felt no responsibility to answer.

Maya continued without asking for input. "Then we took the same confusing premise and applied it to the sex and gender conversation. Some people can reproduce human beings. That is a biological fact. How is sex a social construct if the same premise is true? There are quantifiable differences in the biology of men and women. And again, we created a social structure that perpetuated norms that added a value judgment of men as superior to women. So, that difference is not a social construct—the value judgment of male superiority is."

Maya continued, "I appreciate the premise that we are all the same and we have the desire to fast forward to not judging each other by physical characteristics. But it is confusing to try and make people believe something that is not logical. The coping mechanism is to resist the entire argument and keep us stuck where we are. I just want to see us remove the barriers to allyship that seem to be invisible in this conversation."

Roshunda and Eli felt like innocent bystanders taking in this part of the conversation. They didn't want to interrupt the dialogue and could tell that it was on the verge of getting deep real fast.

Nathan understood where Maya landed in this conversation. He remembered that motherhood was probably a stronger element of her identity than womanhood and he understood how the recent shift in terminology could challenge her in this way. He took another mental pause from the energy of her remarks and reminded himself that he was not here as anyone's spokesperson. He listened intently and finally responded, "These are great questions, Maya. I do not have definitive answers for you. In fact, the freedom to not have or need definitive answers and positions around these issues is exactly what we need most."

Maya replied in a tone that sounded apologetic. "That's OK, Nathan. I am not trying to make you a representative for the trans community. Just know that I did my fair share of googling before I asked."

They all broke into laughter when they realized how appropriate the subliminal reference of "googling" was to "asking your Black friend a question."

Nathan didn't have a strong opinion either way and wasn't about to bet on a race he didn't have a horse in. But he did feel the need to counter Maya's passionate soliloquy with an alternate perspective. "Maya, I understand your point and if I was the PR person for trans rights, I would probably handle it differently. I think the most important point to consider is that the first ask always sounds extreme for any version of human rights until power begins to be conceded, and then we move toward a widely accepted middle. Maybe this is just the first stage of this fight for the right to free expression around gender."

Maya feigned a defeated look and said, "That's possible, Nathan. I can accept that."

Roshunda inserted herself back into the conversation. "Nathan, I have been seeing a version of this question circulating on social media. I grew up in and around white culture and went to a predominately white institution for college. That gave me the opportunity to connect with a massive network of white people. I have lived in white neighborhoods for the majority of my adult life, I've worked with predominantly white people, and studied their behavior. Being light skinned, I have access to circles that I otherwise may not have been invited into. If I feel more connected to white culture, why can't I declare my race as white—basically 'pass' as they call it—and have people treat me as such?"

Nathan sipped in a breath of air. He had been prepared for someone to ask this question. Having heard it before, he was able to admit that he was conflicted about the question. For some people, race is as core to their identity as gender is. He gave himself permission to stand in this intersection clueless and replied, "Roshunda, I hear you. The best response I can think of is that most trans people were not raised by trans people. So, their gender identity is a core innate factor that is not related to societal influences. If you think about Rachel Dolezal and even Michael Jackson, who both tested this theory by trying to live their lives in different skin, I am not sure that they would agree that they truly felt like they were another race in their soul. There may have been benefits that they wanted but their expression was a choice. The point is that most transgender people feel like they have no choice. I am sure you have witnessed how there are few societal benefits to be gained from the trans experience. In fact, the treatment is often quite painful at its core."

Everyone paused to take that in. It felt like there was a level of wisdom and grace embedded in that exchange that needed to be bottled and spread to others.

Roshunda realized it was time to swing the conversation in a different direction. "I heard a great analogy that helped me put sexual orientation, gender identity, and expression into perspective. I want everyone to give me a formula that adds up to seven. I will start. Six plus one. That's me, no one's math major." She looked at Maya who was clearly still in her own world from the Ted Talk she just gave.

"I dunno. Three plus four," Maya replied.

"Good solid answer. Nathan?" Roshunda said, turning to him.

Nathan replied, "Forty-nine divided by seven."

"Great," Roshunda added as she looked directly at Eli.

"Three point five times two," Eli said. It was his first contribution to the conversation, and it came with a subtle reminder that he hadn't said a word since they sat down.

"Of course, you gotta be extra," Roshunda laughed.

Eli continued, sounding a little impatient. "How about you tell us what testing our math skills has to do with anything?"

"My point is this. If the formula for seven represents how we live our lives, for some people that translates into their religious beliefs. Christianity is a six plus one religion. There is no God but ours. There is no way other than what is written in the Bible. Perhaps it is time for us to recognize that our way, our equation is correct—for those who choose it. And there are other options for how people choose to live their lives. Just as you can't tell someone that their equation for seven is wrong, it is equally ridiculous to disrespect the value of their equation." Roshunda paused feeling like she had just dropped the mic.

Everyone bought into her pride and allowed Roshunda to have a different kind of senior moment. Maya understood the assignment, gave her a head nod of approval and said, "That's deep."

Eli jumped back in with his usual punctuation on the conversation. "Thank you guys, for proving me wrong. I remember how anxious I was before I let you guys into my life in this way. I should've known your love wouldn't allow a difference like sexual orientation to threaten our friendship. I love y'all like I love biscuits and gravy."

The conversation eventually morphed beyond deep questions for Nathan. They chimed in with commentary on the Oscar slap. Roshunda commented on the extraordinary demonstration of emotional intelligence from Chris Rock and said, "He is gonna get paid in private when Will Smith pays him not to press criminal charges. And he is gonna get paid again in public when he chooses to talk about it." They shared a collective face palm over the unpredictable nature of the human condition in general.

By the time they left, they knew they had strengthened their friendship. And for all of the ways they were different, at their core—they were all the same.

5

WE SHALL
LIVE IN PEACE
MINIMIZING MICROAGGRESSIONS

Susan felt good about recommending their new Chief Diversity Officer (CDO) to work with Jasmine Luther again. She appreciated the culture work Jasmine started several years ago. But after budget cuts suspended that engagement, it seemed like the organization had moved backwards. It was a way to help them prepare the organization for this new role and help him acclimate to the culture.

Jasmine had to admit that she was a little surprised to find out that her new client, Herman Robinson, was a white male from Tennessee. All her biases flooded to the top of her mind as she examined why her brain expected this person to be a woman of color. Her phone must have been listening to her thoughts because a few days before she agreed to this consulting assignment, a post popped up on her feed with an interesting statistic. It showed that 76 percent of CDOs hired after the summer of 2020 were white. She couldn't help but wonder if this was part of the reason that she found herself bad-mouthing the DEI work that had been done since then.

Jasmine logged into Zoom early and went to refresh her water. She didn't realize that the the waiting room feature had been changed to a password that allows participants to enter and announce themselves. Herman arrived on Zoom five minutes early and seemed ready to launch right into the meeting. "Hey there! So nice to meet you. I'm super excited to be on here with you this morning," he stated.

Although Jasmine appreciated his punctuality, she felt Herman imposed on her preparation time and was a little annoyed by it. She matched the high energy of his warm hello and greeting. "Hi there, it's great to see you on as well. Looks like we're a little earlier than scheduled," she added.

"Yes! I figured it would be good to dive right on in. While I have you…" Jasmine raised a finger, and Herman stopped. She felt like she had to pause him to renegotiate another four minutes before the meeting was set to officially start. The new Zoom world had become just as busy as rushing down the hall from meeting to meeting when working in the office. But Jasmine was adamant about taking control of her calendar and her emotional energy. She needed a minute before jumping into a new conversation with this dude.

When she officially started the conversation, exactly on time, he announced, "I'm sorry if I threw you off. I come from the 'Early is on time. On time is late. And late is not acceptable' school of business operations," he chuckled.

Jasmine took a breath and attempted to be as polite as possible in delivering a response she felt strongly about. "Herman, that is good to know about you. And it is probably equally important for you to know that as a consultant, something would have to be drastically wrong with my business model if I had time to be sitting idle before every scheduled meeting. That doesn't sound very billable to me. So, let's agree that on time will be on time for our meetings." She chose to ignore his suggestion that she was thrown off by his early sign in. He would eventually figure out that it would take more than the likes of him to throw her off.

Beyond the hiccup at the onset, she actually liked Herman. He was a gay man who grew up in a racially diverse neighborhood and cut his teeth in sales, marketing, and business development. She struggled to figure out what education, experience, or expertise he had that would lead him into this role. When she couldn't stand the suspense anymore, she simply asked, "So what brought you into this DEI role?"

He was transparent in his response. "I have a great relationship with Susan, the head of HR, and she thought I would be a good fit for this position based on my passion for it." Jasmine wished she could turn off her camera and go on mute for a private WTF moment. Instead, she smiled, gave the head tilt, and added an *"Oh that's interesting"* response.

A major element of this assignment had just been revealed. Many of the people hired into these roles during the summer of the 2020 emergency response period were placed based on demonstrated or assumed passion, but not necessarily for their expertise. And now, three years later, the predictable cycle of Monday morning quarterbacking had started without any examination of why we ran the wrong plays to begin with. Herman lacked actual qualifications and relevant experience for this role and so her task was to somehow help him be successful in spite of that minor detail. It felt like such a slap in the face to all of the over-qualified diversity professionals who could have done a better job.

She was grateful to be busy. But sometimes she felt like her clients were constantly asking her to solve the wrong problems. She knew that DEI work was important, and she also knew that some of it had limited staying power if these same organizations did not address the underlying issues in their culture.

Her experience showed that most senior leaders really wanted to preserve the status quo and maintained an organizational culture that had inherent barriers to behavior change. No one was holding anyone accountable for new outcomes. She had a true moment of anger when she realized that the outpouring of allyship around racial equity in 2020 was possibly influenced by the COVID effect. Nowhere to go. Nothing to do but watch TV. Lingering pain from so many deaths accidentally channeled into empathy for George Floyd.

Jasmine had the painful realization that we were inside with nothing else to do but watch his murder over and over again. The development of this ounce of empathy had already run out and those same people had the nerve to now be experiencing "empathy fatigue". The term itself sounded crazy. More recently, the narrative that all of the work done in the past three years has been a waste of time and money was becoming more prevalent. All the while the majority of people in those roles have no vested interest in creating racial equity.

Jasmine grabbed her iPad and made a few notes to address with Jim at their next meeting. She stopped herself before she became too despondent about the actual state of affairs and switched her focus back to the task at hand and what she could actually control. She finished the plan for Herman .

> **1. Onboarding Plan:** help Herman plan his first one hundred days, first six months up to his first year, with milestones attached to each one

Jasmine had a template for this critical step that needed to be customized based on the organization specifics and Herman's learning style.

> **2. Culture Assessment:** gain a full understanding of the organizational culture and the ways it supports and hinders the business goal

This step was also important to inform the details of where DEI fit into the equation. Her experience was that most organizations embark on DEI as a disease to cure without realizing that DEI is a symptom of a health or illness within an organization. She still needed to figure out if this organization was serious about this work or if she was about to be an Organizational Development (OD) ho—just in it for the money.

3. Priority Focus Area: identify and articulate
through strategic communication plan

Jasmine preferred for this to emerge from the data collected in the assessment. But Herman was adamant that he wanted to tackle microaggressions as his burning platform. Jasmine wasn't opposed to it as she understood the importance of solving for this experience as an indicator of a healthy culture. Her problem was that Herman seemed to want to go for the brightest shiny object that would get him a quick win without any strategic consideration.

Jasmine made notes for her conversation to sell this focus and outline a plan to address microaggressions. She could hear herself talking through it as her words hit the page.

1. Understand the challenges that make people not want to return to the office.
   - Beyond the obvious convenience of being home, people with each diversity element experienced different benefits of being home:
     - The data suggest that Black/African Americans appreciated not having to process through George Floyd's killing while having the burden of white colleagues' comfort.

- □ Women reported being better able to manage child and elder care and additional household responsibilities.
- □ People with disabilities didn't have to put up with strangers petting their service animal or asking intrusive questions about their accommodations.
- □ Jews and Muslims could manage their prayer schedule and religious needs more discreetly.
- □ People with neurodiversities could manage the lighting and other elements to support how they process information.

- Share examples of microaggression.

2. Use The Return to the Office initiative as a natural reset point to focus on our interactions with each other.
   - Anchor initiative in existing values around internal behavior and established or desired organizational culture.
   - Extract key learnings from culture assessment to inform the broader approach.
     - □ Jasmine thought that Herman wanted to skip this step, but she added it to the list so that she could stay in integrity to the process.
   - Work with leaders to ensure that they have an opportunity to be immersed in this initiative before it is rolled out.
   - Create communication campaign with attachment to a bigger purpose.
   - Provide training on microaggressions that includes connection to values, organizational culture, and shared expectations.
   - Monitor outcomes closely, reward affirming behaviors, and penalize damaging behaviors consistently.

As a first step to prepare leaders, Herman invited Jasmine to the leadership retreat and planned a Fireside Chat style opportunity for him to interview her. He felt that introducing the topic in a non-threatening way would help engage senior leaders on the behaviors that many of them needed to change. Jasmine recognized the standard focus on white comfort as a necessary part of every initiative. It caused her to wonder if Herman had that unique quality that every CDO needs to demonstrate in this role: the willingness to challenge the status quo and push people to have new behaviors. If the desire to be liked was stronger than their internal compass set toward progress, Herman and the rest of them would fail.

Herman was almost giddy on the day of the event. He launched the Fireside Chat with a brief overview of Jasmine's credentials and how much he had enjoyed working with her for their first three months together.

At the start, he said, "Jasmine is here to help us understand the context of the Microaggressions Initiative that I have been socializing and, more specifically, how we can change our own behavior to be better role models in the organization. We know this won't happen overnight, but it is possible if we all try."

The red lights started flashing and the sirens were almost deafening in Jasmine's head. She hated nothing more than the weak ass language that was often used to introduce DEI initiatives. Letting people off the hook before they even got started was a dog whistle for "*We are all just pretending to care about this shit. We don't expect to succeed but have to look like we are trying.*" Even use of the word "try" was troubling in a room full of highly compensated adults. She ignored all of it and responded with a big smile and a warm, "Thanks so much for having me, Herman." She had an instant headache.

"We know you have a lot of questions, and this is the place to get them answered. Even the uncomfortable ones. Let's start with the definition of microaggression: those subtle things that people say, imply, or do that communicate something hostile, derogatory, or negative to someone from a historically marginalized or excluded group," Herman explained. "Jasmine, you have an interesting spin on the term microaggression." He turned to her, giving her the floor. Herman was anxious to have her share this first point exactly as they had done in the dry run.

"Yes, the term Microaggression is actually a microaggression in and of itself because it assumes that the infraction is small. Neither the experience nor the impact is miniscule. So, the first thing I want to start with is that there is a shift happening where microaggressions are being reframed from the perspective of the offender to the perspective of the offended person." Jasmine paused to gauge how well this first point would land. She knew that if they struggled with this key learning, it would be a long and painful afternoon.

"I want to highlight the term 'historically marginalized or excluded group.' This was new to me. Can you tell us a little bit more about how that term is being used now?" Herman asked.

Jasmine was happy to jump into a question that could serve as a softball entry into a deeper discussion. "Yes, sure. The term minority is both factually incorrect and diminishing in many ways. Demographics suggest that the basis for categorizing someone as a minority is shifting. More importantly, the connotation of the word means 'less than.' Therefore, DEI language is evolving to terms that are more accurate and empowering," Jasmine said now as she faced Herman.

Herman continued. "Can you give us an example of a microaggression?"

Jasmine replied. "Yes, I will share two of them. The first one is mine. I'm the offender," she said as she pointed to herself. "When I go to the grocery store, I do like most people. I do a quick scan and make a totally biased decision on which cashier I think will get me though checkout the fastest. So, last week I made my selection and as I started to put my groceries on the belt, I looked up at the cashier, attempted to make small talk, and said, 'Hi, how are you doing?' After she responded 'Fine,' I continued with, 'So, when are you due?' As soon as the question left my mouth, I realized how inappropriate it was. The look on her face switched my thinking and gave me a full range of options that made my question so inappropriate."

Jasmine could tell her audience wasn't following and she needed to further elaborate. "What was it about my narrow view of body size that made me make that assumption of body size? What if she had a tumor? Or if she had been trying to have children and couldn't? I snapped out of embarrassment and tried to recover by saying 'I am so sorry. What I should have said was—you sure are getting this line through quickly. That's why I chose you.' She rolled her eyes and I realized that we don't always get or deserve the other person's absolution for microaggressions. I also share my example so that you know that this is a universal experience. No one is expected to be perfect in the area of understanding other people's experiences. But you are expected to be actively involved in learning compassion."

Jasmine paused and absorbed the head nods around the room. When they looked like they were ready for more, she continued, "The second example is a microaggression I heard from a young, biracial lawyer. She tells the story of walking into court, she's got her briefcase, she's getting ready to do a deposition, and she's one of the first to arrive. She puts her briefcase on the table and the court reporter says to her, 'Do you know when the lawyers will arrive?'"

Herman acknowledged someone with their hand up as Jasmine provided the example. He didn't want for anyone to misunderstand any points and acknowledged their question. "Go ahead Sven," he said.

"Aren't we going a bit overboard with this stuff? That was just an honest question. Isn't all of this Woke Movement BS hurting our business?" Sven said. He sat back in his chair as if he had just dropped the mic and established a new direction for the conversation.

Jasmine noticed Susan cringing in her seat as an indication that this was the resident asshole who was probably running rampant as the biggest offender in the group. Jasmine replied by first thanking Sven for his question and giving her opportunity to make two important follow-up points. She started with, "Would the question have made sense if she was a white male?"

His silence became a clue that he was accustomed to throwing verbal grenades and getting a rise out of people. Jasmine didn't plan to go down this road, but she had eaten her Wheaties that day. She ignored his nonresponse and launched into part 1B of her response. "Let's examine the impact of the question because this is the new focus for the understanding of and responses to microaggressions. The assumption that this person could not possibly be a lawyer is condescending. The inability to ascribe professional recognition despite all of the context clues is a reflection of how bias suspends common sense in otherwise intelligent people. And minimizing her identity in a context where identity matters for successful outcomes, for example, the ability to be convincing in court, is a long-standing tactic that has an adverse impact on members of historically excluded groups."

Jasmine paused and allowed a moment for questions, objections, and rebuttals. Hearing none, she continued, "Let's explore that concept of 'Woke BS' for a minute." She shifted in her seat before she continued. "There has been a suspicious and strategic co-opting of the term 'woke' that has made it unnecessarily complicated and negatively associated with standard Golden Rule behaviors. The term 'woke' still means what it has always meant—awake, not asleep.

The colloquial use of the term was coined to mean no longer sleeping or ignoring issues related to Black Lives Matter. This became specifically relevant to address the millions of people for whom George Floyd's torture and subsequent death was their 'wake-up' call to allyship. Many 2020 allies claimed to 'not have been aware' of the true issues surrounding racial equity until that moment. And hence, the term 'woke' came back into the vernacular. In other words, stop hitting the snooze button and ignoring what is going on around racial injustice. That's it. It's that simple. We need to stop making it more complicated than it needs to be." Jasmine allowed her tone to provide the necessary punctuation.

She took a deep breath and continued, "The new use of the term in legislation is a strategy to deflect the power of this awakening that ultimately leads to critical mass of allyship and reconciliatory behaviors. Problems are never solved until people wake up to the existence of the problem and commit to solutions. So rather than create false confusion over semantics, you could just say that you prefer the status quo and want to stay asleep. Because that is what everyone understands from the BS being offered now." Jasmine used a short pause as a lifeline to help Sven save face.

Sven sat back in his chair as Jasmine made eye contact. He acknowledged he had no bark in this fight and gave a slight head nod to Jasmine to continue. "Here's what I want you to know about that microaggression example I shared a moment ago. It is from Cheslie Kryst's, Miss USA 2019, last TikTok video before she committed suicide. She was explaining her decision to transition from her career as a lawyer to become a journalist. As painful as it is, the reason I am sharing it with you is because it alludes to a bigger point about the potentially dangerous cumulative effect of these 'little things.'" Jasmine exaggerated the obnoxious air quotes gesture to make her point.

Herman jumped back in. His heart was racing, and he expected at least two or three follow-up questions and/or phone calls about that one moment. He changed his tone to an upbeat indication that this was the last question. "So Jasmine, what can we as senior leaders do to be better role models in this regard?"

Jasmine returned to her delightful voice and provided a bulleted list with warm additions of reassuring narratives.

1. Reframe your thinking from a constant focus on your frame of reference. Expand your approach to include a version of reality from the other person's perspective. I realize that is difficult when you may only have lived experience in your majority body. But it is worthwhile to learn how others experience the world and why these constant insults are harmful.

2. Learn more about the conditions that create microaggressions. For example, immerse yourself in content from multiple news sources, diverse thought leaders on social media, and attend ERG events at your organizations. These are three great sources for new perspectives that are absolutely free to you.

3. Prepare to be corrected and manage your ego as you respond. Get comfortable with the idea that others, even your subordinates in the organization, will begin to push back. The pandemic has changed us and how much we are willing to tolerate at work. If someone corrects you, listen attentively and plan on exercising humility in your response.

4. Learn new skills. One of the things you will learn in our upcoming training is how to issue an effective apology when you are the offender. There is an actual formula and I highly recommend you follow it to the letter in the early stages of skill building.

5. Practice micro-affirmations. Find ways to enhance your

interactions by positively affirming others. A few examples that you can implement immediately include:

- consider additional religious holidays and observances beyond the traditional Christian calendar when scheduling
- get familiar with the names, including correct pronunciation, and faces of employees and use them when you interact
- assume that everyone you see belongs in every room you see them in

Herman applauded Jasmine. "Well, that is all the time we have for today. Thank you so much for being with us Jasmine. Before you all go, I wanted to do two more things. First, remind you all that you will be among the first to go through the organization-wide training on microaggressions. You will see three invitations pop up in your calendar. Accept the one that works best for you and decline the others. Please make time to attend. You will want to be in the know on what all employees will be learning in these sessions. We need skills and tools to address and combat microaggressions. Then, when the training is over, we will reconvene for a group coaching session to unpack our learnings and share our action plans. And secondly, I want to share this beautiful quote I saw on a bumper sticker. '*In order for us to live in peace, we must understand what peace means for others.*' Have a great day everyone."

While Jasmine entertained the standard thank yous and attaboys at the end of the meeting, she could not help but wonder if this assignment would end up being window dressing or a rock through a window to effect change.

6

DEEP IN
MY HEART

LOVING RELATIONSHIPS

LaToya and Shane were living their best lives together in LA. However, it was starting to feel like their individual best did not include each other. They continued to cheer each other on like Denzel Washington celebrating his wife Pauletta, but the weight of their schedules was starting to make them feel isolated inside the relationship. It was almost as if the need and desire for success had become more important than the need and desire for each other.

Shane first became aware of this while LaToya was on a five-day work trip in Europe. She called when she arrived, and he was glad to know that she had arrived safely. But after not hearing from her for two days, he felt that maybe he needed to reach out. He monitored the time zones and texted, "Hey Babe. How are you doing?"

About six hours later, LaToya finally replied. "I'm good. Just exhausted. We are on the go nonstop. How are you doing?"

Shane paused, looked at the phone, and tried to resist the urge to be in his feelings about how sterile the message sounded. Instead of texting, he dialed her knowing it was 7:00 p.m. over there.

LaToya answered right away. "Hey Shane," she said in a warm welcoming tone.

Despite her tone, she sounded off. She said, *Shane.* Shane? Not honey or babe? Something about being called by his name felt funny. "Hey Babe," he deliberately replied. He paused to see if she would reciprocate, but she allowed his name to hang out with her silence. After not getting his usual term of endearment, he continued, "I'm just checking to make sure they aren't working you too hard."

"Nah, I'm good. What's going on?" she asked.

"Nothing special. I just wanted to hear your voice," Shane said.

"OK then, I will call you back when I get to the hotel and get settled for bed," LaToya responded, her words clipped.

Shane perked up at the idea that LaToya planned to make time for him that evening. "Ooh OK! Milk and cookies on Zoom before bed!" Shane ended the call feeling like a teenager whose date just said yes for the prom.

LaToya didn't specify what time she'd call. And he wasn't sure when to expect her back in the hotel. So, that night he waited. And waited. Eventually, he fell asleep and woke up the next morning with a feeling of emptiness from no missed calls. Instead, she sent a text that read, "Can't keep my eyes open. Will ping you tomorrow."

Shane began questioning himself. *When did I get so sensitive?* His thoughts had started to sound like some girlfriend bullshit that women say to each other when their man is on his grind and doesn't have time to spend every waking moment with her. *What is happening to me?*

He understood the stress of them both trying to prove themselves at their new jobs. In addition, they were both caring for elderly parents and trying to be the kind of children they would want their children to be someday. In addition, they both aspired to entrepreneurship and put in late nights researching and trying to build their personal brands into a viable professional brand that could be leveraged in the marketplace. He and LaToya were both very good at understanding the hustle mentality and until now, his yearning for his woman had been laid at the altar of being the quintessential supportive partner. But today felt different.

The experience of feeling disconnected had been happening for a while so Shane knew this was not a fleeting moment. This time he decided to sit in the discomfort and sort through the facts to decide how he felt. After doing a mental rewind of LaToya's behavior and comparing it to the normal cheating clues, Shane took infidelity off the table. She had that deep love that was more likely to have trouble letting go than cheat on her man. She truly just had too much on her plate. She was appropriately engrossed in her career. She was winning in so many ways, and this was her season to enjoy the accolades that she had worked so hard for. Nothing about him or how he was feeling wanted to stifle that in any way.

In fact, it made him even more certain that he wanted to give her the last Infinity Stone that society uses as validation, the ring.

What Shane didn't know was that LaToya woke up feeling guilty that she hadn't spoken to him before bed like she said she would. She knew how important it was to have their "we time" when she was away. She just didn't have it in her last night. In fact, she was starting to feel like she was disappointing him more and more lately. For a brief moment, she explored the possibility that he wasn't providing the type of support that she needed either. Was he starting to get in his feelings about her success? God forbid, was he starting to compete with her? She resisted the urge to go down that rabbit hole and snapped herself back to personal account-ability for what had been going on in their relationship.

She remembered Kevin Samuels and the kind of conversations he sparked. She actually agreed with many of the things he said about women needing to take more responsibility for their behavior and how they show up in relationships. This was also true for men, and the ways they needed to step up their game. It sounded like the types of things she said to her little brother when he made poor choices in women. She felt strongly that the biggest problem with KS was that he was an internet sensation without any of the real training or adherence to ethics that certified coaches and counseling professionals go through. So here he was with all his personal trauma and baggage, giving advice recklessly in a brash style (really designed to get attention rather than heal others) to impressionable men and women who mistakenly saw him as a professional.

The feeling of being physically and emotionally exhausted was starting to feel like a new way of life for LaToya. She heard that depression was a lingering side effect of COVID, and she was starting to think that there was something to that for her. But this was way more than lingering COVID sadness. It was more than the usual trauma of seeing all the ways our community is marginalized and even gunned down in grocery stores. It was way more than the stress of being back in the office after a year and a half of peace and productivity at home. It was her—her body just didn't feel the same. Her hair had just started regaining the thickness it once had. Then she remembered a conversation she overheard at the hairdresser.

A woman in her forties was starting to have the types of complaints that LaToya used to hear the aunties talk about. The new term was perimenopause, when women are in the early stages of menopause. She began researching and found out that it is far more prevalent than anyone ever talked about.

All of a sudden LaToya felt a wave of grief come over her. She missed her mother so much. She longed for all of the lessons her mother did not get time to teach her. Details about menopause were just the tip of the iceberg. She allowed herself the gift of tears and sat in sadness until she knew she had less than thirty minutes to meet her colleagues in the lobby.

At that point, she wished she had the license to exhibit the type of vulnerability that Brené Brown writes about. Today would be a day when she would call in sad. She would say:

"I'm struggling today, and I just can't bring myself to put on a brave face and majority mannerisms to show up as the strong overachiever you expect me to be. I want you to pretend that today is one of those days within the first ninety days of George Floyd's death when it finally felt OK for us to say, 'we are not OK'. Today I need for you to not pimp my potential by expecting more of me than you do of others and then minimizing my rewards relative to others. Today, I need you to treat me the way you treat white women—as fragile beings worthy of your empathy and protection. Today I want you to allow me to operate in my feminine energy instead of putting masculine expectations on me."

As awesome as it would be to have the conditions aligned enough to say that out loud, she realized that today was not the day. She had always said that someday she would sign up for counseling and get a therapist. Today was the day for that. She went into her phone and set a reminder to make an appointment.

It took more than a minute of sitting in the discomfort, but Shane finally got the point that seemed so obvious from jump. He was feeling like LaToya needed career validation more than she needed his love and affection. Regardless of if he was right or wrong, the feeling was the thing to address. It is not about where your significant other falls on your priority list, it is about how they make you feel. Is it possible to be third on each other's list (after demanding jobs and elderly parents) and still feel like number one?

He felt like he had a whole series of podcasts playing in his head that were being cross-referenced with cigar room conversations with fraternity brothers and autopsies of past relationships. He concluded that the concept of submission was overused and played out. The men he knew don't really want submission. They want to feel respected. He distinctly remembered hearing Pastor Keion Henderson say that "Love is a woman's big word. Most men don't ask women to love them. They ask you to respect them. Because to us, psychologically when women respect us, we automatically feel loved. That plane lands on two different runways." Shane made a note to himself to save that YouTube video for LaToya.

He realized that it is easier for white women to show up as more willing to submit to men is because society relieves them of the burden of striving for significance. They get to operate in a system where they constantly receive personal and collective validation. The orientation to submissiveness is exponentially easier when the world treats you like a damsel in distress all the time. The curse of the strong Black woman is that everyone treats you like a man.

Shane had listened in to enough conversations with his mother, aunties, sisters, and cousins to agree that Black women just need an uninterrupted opportunity to trust and respect their men again. The scholars have been saying it for years and he thought it is still true that men and women need to work together to restore the damage done by the legacy of slavery, and the subsequent laws and approaches that perpetuate its effects. There are so many layers of damage to our relationships that the qualities one person needs from the other person are struggling to emerge.

Deep in his heart, Shane knew he loved LaToya and he wanted to spend the rest of his life with her. The issue he was wrestling with was his interior conflict and ulterior motives.

His interior conflict was that marriage is the most expensive bet a man places. If it hits, the payout is huge. You get the emotional benefit of lifetime partnership, financial benefit of being a power couple, and building generational wealth together. Not to mention the aspirational benefit of being sexually satisfied by the same person for the rest of your life.

Shane realized that if you choose the wrong person or that person changes in ways that now conflict with your needs—you're screwed. Beyond the emotional devastation of losing your partner, you now have to contend with the possibility of losing half of what you worked so hard for. Even worse than that, your relationship with your kids hinges on her maturity and willingness to allow you to be an awesome father even when she can't see you as an awesome husband. The risk of the relationship you have with the love of your life transforming into the war of a lifetime felt like the one battle zone Shane was truly afraid of. Instantly he wondered if LaToya would be open to a prenup.

Shane created an honest bulleted list of conclusions in his head:

- He knew that Black men tend to need more evidence of personal stability than white men in the corporate world. So, he did not want his decision to marry LaToya to be influenced by this knowledge in any way.

- In his last men's group meeting, they were discussing how few single Black men make it to C-suite roles compared to heterosexual single white men or gay Black men. So being married afforded him the benefit of being seen as a committed family man and therefore one step closer to psychological parity with his white counterparts.

- The irony is that this dynamic existed even in light of his military experience. Many of his peers had never even been a Boy Scout compared to his twenty-two years as a US Marine. The thought of being measured against a subpar yardstick felt like a punch in the gut every Monday morning.

- He also acknowledged that LaToya's accomplishments made her far more than a trophy wife. He could leave her at the punch bowl of any work event and not worry about her embarrassing him. In fact, he could come back and be in consideration for a promotion. Her humble brag skills were impeccable, and he loved all the ways she stroked his ego in private and in public.

By the end of the list, he felt like the decision had been made. He knew that LaToya was his person, and that marriage was the next step for them. He would make it his priority to get their love back on track by practicing the kind of commitment marriage requires. It's funny how as soon as you get married you are no longer 'engaged.' He wanted a relationship where they were engaged for the rest of their lives. Date night did not have to be every Friday night. And the cuddle up did not have to happen only on Sunday morning. But he took on the determination of a soldier going into battle to get his woman back from any personal or societal conditions that were trying to take her from him. He committed himself to making sure they both felt connected in every moment regardless of the life responsibilities they were engaged in.

Shane reminded himself of the pet names he and LaToya had for each other: Thunder and Lightning. Thunder is created when lightning passes through the air. And that was them, an interconnected force of nature.

LaToya had a long flight home to consider what was going on with her and Shane.

In addition to feeling disconnected on this trip, they were at the awkward point in their relationship where being introduced in corporate settings as a 'girlfriend' or 'boyfriend' didn't feel like a match anymore. She didn't want to rush Shane into marriage just because of social norms, but she had started to feel like something was shifting in their relationship. She couldn't help but notice that women seemed to get career rewards when they were single because it appears that they have more time and emotional energy to dedicate to their company. Once they marry, people start mapping their fertility against business goals and suddenly, you aren't considered for key roles anymore because you might go off on maternity leave. One of her cousins kept her marriage a secret for six months while she was being considered for a rotational program. After she got accepted, she started wearing her wedding ring at work. Once again, we find ourselves playing the game until we slay the game.

LaToya remembered one of her favorite episodes from the Recruit for Love, Retain for a Lifetime Series. She pulled up the notes in her phone and began scrolling.

Her analytical mind enjoyed the framework they offered with areas of compatibility that both parties should consider.

1. Life Energy: the degree of compatibility in multiple areas of life.
   - Sexual energy: the degree of physical attraction. Potential to meet each other's needs in bed. Most relationships start and flourish here without consideration of the next four areas.
   - Lifestyle compatibility: ability to fit into each other's career and social circle.
   - Work schedule: 9-5, shift work, or entrepreneurs with flexibility.
   - Socioeconomic level: dictates lifestyle choices.

- Spending patterns: do they spend on things (designer handbag) or experiences (trip)? Are they practical or extravagant?

2. Mental Compatibility: ability to stimulate each other intellectually. Everyone may not have this overtly on their list, but some people have a high need for a mental sparring partner or they get bored. Many instances of cheating start here. One partner goes looking for or stumbles upon mental stimulation that is not present at home. Because this is a core element of attraction, they end up in a sexual relationship as that is part of their intimacy pattern.

3. Emotional Compatibility: ability to meet each other's emotional needs.
   - Validation and admiration: struggles if partner is aloof.
   - Positive energy: struggles if partner is pessimistic or suffers from depression.
   - Emotional connectivity: struggles if partner isn't tapped into their emotions.
   - Loyalty and commitment: struggles if status is ambiguous.
   - Depth: struggles with superficial connections.
   - Space to socialize: struggles if partner is clingy and critical of their social life.

4. Family Compatibility: potential for families to blend smoothly; influenced by in-laws, stepchildren, and their ages.

5. Spiritual Compatibility: degree to which your spiritual ideals blend peacefully.

As LaToya read through her notes, she began to dissect her relationship with Shane.

6. Their sexual chemistry was through the roof from the moment they met. It wasn't until she started studying astrology that she understood what it meant to have conjunctions like Mars and Pluto as well as Moon and Venus. It felt like they hit the synastry lottery and people commented on how they showed up in a room like soulmates.

7. For the most part, their lifestyles were compatible. Shane was a very generous provider, but she always made sure to let him know that her career and earning power was important to her. Even after having kids, she would always be a working mom. LaToya knew she had expensive taste, but she was raised to make sure that she could always finance her tastes. She also made a point to demonstrate that she had Shane's back financially. He appreciated it so much when she secretly made the last ten payments of his student loan.

8. Mentally they complemented each other. She respected that Shane was an undercover Smart Brotha who didn't feel the need to hit people over the head with his intellect. His emotional intelligence was off the chart, and he could engage her problem-solving skills better than anyone she had ever been with. She had a moment of pause and wondered how he was experiencing her in this area.

9. That line of questioning caused her to also question if she was meeting his emotional needs. She understood that Black men need to come home to women who help heal the

wounds that the workplace inflicts. She and her girlfriends had begun to be more self-reflective about the ways their behavior actually validates the angry Black woman stereotype at home. As hard as it was to face this reality, LaToya recommitted herself to paying more attention to how she tuned into Shane's emotional needs and picked up on the clues he left.

For example, if he texted her more than twice on a particular thought during the day, he probably wanted to debrief about it later. If he laid on the couch with the blanket around him, he probably wanted to cuddle with her but she was busy doing something else. When he fed her food at the dinner table, it meant that he needed something else in her mouth.

10. LaToya knew that family compatibility was a layup in the grand scheme of things. Shane's family loved LaToya and her family loved him. There were no issues here except the minor issues of shade his mother threw from time to time. Even that she didn't take seriously. It was just the side effect of dating a Black woman's only son.

11. LaToya knew that spirituality also felt beautifully aligned. She and Shane were both Christians at their core with very different levels of expression. He maintained the religious practice of always saying grace before he ate, making time to attend church, and participating in the worship experience and men's ministry activities. LaToya considered herself a more spiritual person who used texts as reference, was open to various spiritual practices, and was using astrology to understand herself and her life at a deeper

level. Day by day, moment by moment, they understood the cliché that "the family that prays together stays together."

LaToya felt the need to add one more thing: racial compatibility. All relationships should consider if and how racial differences and similarities factor into personal interactions.

In that moment, LaToya realized that the analysis was complete. Her analytical side, prone to over-thinking, had what it needed. Deep in her heart, she was ready to let go of old conditioning about being an independent woman. She had checked all the boxes on taking care of herself. She did the work to understand and love herself. She was getting better at acknowledging and apologizing when the challenging parts of her personality reared their ugly head. And now she felt ready to surrender her heart to the man who had proven himself worthy of that surrender.

LaToya was excited to be home in Shane's arms after her Europe trip. With the reflection she had done, she was ready to address and resolve their relationship issues to build a foundation for the future. He seemed exceptionally chatty on the drive home from the airport. That usually meant there would be few words once they walked in the door. Shane's body longed for LaToya before she even got into the car. He had so much to tell her about what had happened at work and in his life over the past week. He had dinner and all the accessories necessary to have the conversation that had been brewing for so long. The dating and deciding was over. He always knew that someday he would find the right woman and lock her down as his wife for life. Someday was today.

7

THE TRUTH SHALL
SET US FREE

WHITE MALE ACCOUNTABILITY

As Jim prepared for the CEO Consortium meeting, he began to think about how much he enjoyed being a part of this group. It was born during the COVID-19 crisis when a group of CEOs decided to get together to brainstorm the challenges they were having, and share solutions. Of the fifty-four official members, there was a broad range of industries represented and some racial diversity. But for the most part, it was still more homogeneous than he would have liked.

What Jim appreciated most was the degree of trust that was built between the CEOs and the strict code of silence that was established so they knew they could speak candidly. Everything that happened in these sessions was closed. There were no recordings, and you would be expelled if you were found to repeat anything outside of the meetings.

Everyone arrived early and used the initial ten to fifteen minutes to meet, greet, and connect with others. Jim could not help but notice that none of the normal Black and brown members had arrived yet. There was always at least three to five people of color in attendance. It wasn't until he checked his phone and noticed the date that he realized they scheduled the meeting on the Juneteenth holiday. Jim decided to scan the email thread discussing this meeting. He saw where someone asked to reschedule this meeting because it was a holiday. To which, someone replied, "That's the best reason to keep it on the calendar. We won't have to take up another valuable day from our schedule."

It made perfect sense why they were not there. Maybe they were offended by the reply and decided not to attend at all. Jim realized he missed an opportunity to be an ally and without those members at the table, he suspected the discussion itself would not be as rich as it normally was.

After the assigned lead kicked off the meeting and asked for input on the agenda, Jim decided to put his concern on the record. "We missed an important scheduling note. Today is Juneteenth, and I don't know if that's the reason that some of our other members are not here. But it kind of feels like turning the clock back to be sitting here as a group with no visible racial diversity."

An older white male responded quickly. "Well, you know, if you ask me, I kind of like it like this because always having to be on my P's and Q's with this woke bullshit pushed down my throat is really starting to get on my nerves. So, maybe we can just have a good solid meeting with just us."

Everyone paused as if to take the emotional temperature in the room and see if this was really a problem. Jim was genuinely interested in the man's response. He glanced at his name tag to address him. "Tell me more about that, David. I want to make sure that I understand," he said as he shifted his weight in his seat preparing for what he knew would be a hot discussion.

"Come on Jim. Let's be honest about this shit for once. I have tried to get on board with this diversity and inclusion stuff. And when it comes to veterans and people with disabilities I can actually get there. But this whole conversation about race has just gone too far. It feels like they want to take over and if we aren't careful, there won't be any jobs left for us or our children while we make space for them. Don't you ever long for the good old days when you knew what to expect in the workplace?"

Jim could hardly believe what he was hearing out loud. Despite the rage he wanted to express, he decided to take the high road and participate in a potentially futile teachable moment. "So, this is your honest opinion? You aren't just being contrary for conversation's sake?"

Others nodded their heads in agreement as if to send a deliberate message of consensus. Another member spoke up. "I actually feel stifled. Like I am not allowed to express my opinion, but they are free to express their opinions."

There was a huge round of nods and verbal agreements.

"So let me be sure I understand. What exactly would you prefer to see regarding race in the workplace?" Jim could feel the blood rushing to his head, and he felt the need to give one more opportunity for someone to jump out of the bushes and declare that he was being punked.

"I think that we are going overboard with the diversity and inclusion rhetoric," another person jumped in. "Our forefathers created an infrastructure that works. It built America into the superpower that it is today. Why are we trying to turn it upside down? We have already made tons of progress and yet they want more? I feel like they won't stop until we are the ones who are oppressed."

Jim repositioned himself in his chair, now sitting fully upward. "So, you acknowledge that oppression has occurred?"

"Well, yeah. But life ain't fair," said David. He chuckled smugly and his casual dismissal of racial trauma seemed to be the official death of DEI initiatives around the world.

Jim had had enough of this charade where he pretended to sit and entertain the level of bigotry he was hearing. He had collected all the data he needed for a few of his own personal decisions and he was ready to speak his peace and then let his absence be his statement.

When no one chimed in, he continued, "The new use of the term in legislation is a strategy to deflect the power of this awakening that ultimately leads to allyship and reconciliatory behaviors. Problems are never solved until people wake up to the existence of the problem and commit to solutions. So rather than create false confusion over semantics, just say that you prefer the status quo and want to stay asleep. Because we have lost all credibility with what we are saying and doing now."

David jumped back in to try and rescue the moment. "Jim, come on. It's not that serious. We have businesses to run. Shareholders to consider. Certainly, you don't expect any of us to take bread out of our own mouths to give to a group who wouldn't know what to do with reparations even if you gave it to them." He looked at the others for collective validation of his last point.

Jim stood up and shook his head. "OK, I have had enough. I expected so much more from each of you. This is exactly the kind of disgusting thought process that they are accusing us of. And then we try to convince them that we are good people, who just don't know how to do equality. And to be quite honest, it sounds like we are not. What you all are actually saying is that the only vision of America that you want is one where you have your knee on somebody's neck. That is who you are presenting yourself as. And I am scared that you are not able to operate in a version of America where people have equal opportunity. It doesn't matter that most of you will still keep your senior level positions. Nobody here is at risk of losing anything. You sound like James Patterson, the best-selling author talking about how hard it is for older white male writers. Your children are not at risk of losing anything, but what you're saying is you don't necessarily want your children or grandchildren to be operating on a level playing field. What you want is for them to continue to have the advantages that they already have, and you are determined to maintain that status quo. The quintessential expression of privilege is when you interpret equality as oppression. You are resisting the concept of equality in favor of the traditional demonstrations of preference in your favor."[2]

David became adamant, "So what is wrong with us looking out for ourselves and our children?"

Jim didn't miss a beat in responding, "We better find a way to look out for everyone's children. If we do not face the fact that white supremacy is not sustainable—there won't be an America for us to rule over. We will simply have destroyed ourselves from the inside out. And even our biggest enemies will always have an advantage over us because at the end of the day when they say Russian or they say Korean, they literally mean everybody."

One of the female executives jumped in and said, "OK wait a minute, Jim. I get what you are saying but there are so many battles to fight. I think the point is that everyone is just trying to make things easier for them in their group. As a white woman, I struggle with—."

Jim deliberately interrupted her by waving his hand, dismissing the normal stereotypes that would be associated with his rudeness. "Jesus Francine. I can't with the fragile white woman plea right now. Let me just remind you that society continues to put you at the center of DEI, and you and your peers are doing more harm than good most days. Just let me finish." She sat back in her chair and picked up her phone in a subtle attempt to match microaggression for microaggression. In the moment, Jim realized that he had just punished a colleague for his inability to verbalize those sentiments to his wife.

---

2   https://www.youtube.com/watch?v=mGUEcEwRtNg.

"Let me explain what I see as the future of racial equity in America. If we don't embrace a version of America that is equitable, we will jeopardize our position and credibility altogether." Jim readied himself to dive in but could tell he would be met with resistance. Francine had redirected her attention to her phone and the others appeared uncomfortable, but Jim proceeded.

"There are three things that we can expect in the future of racial equity. First the continued resistance to racial equity that we have seen in America is going to continue. As a country, in our organizations, and as individuals, we only solve problems that we want to solve. When bottles of water became a problem after 9/11, we solved it by prohibiting water bottles through security at airports. But when it comes to racial equity, there is this overarching resistance to solving this problem. Can you think of any other problems that it doesn't seem like we want to solve?" David said, "my nephew was killed in a school shooting so I am well aware that gun violence is not high on our national priority list." Jim's facial expression changed and he expressed regret by responding, "Wow, David, I am so sorry that has hit so close to home for you and your family."

After a long pause, Jim continued, "the second thing we can expect to see going forward is a natural crumbling that has been occurring slowly over time. We all know the issue of birth rates and how demographics are changing. The notion of birth rates disrupting the perceived balance of power is colloquially known as 'The Browning of America.' The white population perceives itself as losing ground in both numbers and power. But let's be honest here, this is an irrational fear. By every other indicator there really has been no decline in power. Because based on the trends of behavior, we have no reason to believe than an increase in the numbers of people of color in America is going to change the operation of America. But what's happening is that the number of allies is growing, and their confidence is growing. When the number of allies and confidence grows, that is what will contribute to the crumbling. And soon, the system that holds racism in place will crumble naturally. If that doesn't happen fast enough, we will find out that Shirley Chisholm's advice will take hold. 'If they don't give you a seat at the table, bring a folding chair.' And it won't be used to sit quietly," Jim paused to assess the room. He knew these were difficult messages that many in this group had never heard before but somehow today didn't feel like the day to be diplomatic.

"And my last point…the future of racial equity is a redesigned version. As I noted before, the demographics are changing. Millennials are not just in higher numbers in organizations, but they are actually moving up the ranks in position of power. The way they behave will begin to impact the results we see. Millennials grew up in the era of social media. Therefore, they have the exposure to a larger audience. With that exposure, they acted. Remember when millennials told us we don't have to come into the office every day? And look at us now. COVID has proven the exact point they were making. Millennials are changing our views." Jim stopped to catch his breath.

Everyone in the room was split. Half were taking what he said seriously, and the other half seemed deliberately disconnected. Jim felt discouraged, as he took a deep sigh. "Like job descriptions?" someone shouted from the back.

"What's that?" Jim asked as he scanned the room to see who was speaking.

"Job descriptions," a young millennial repeated. "Employers are redesigning outdated job descriptions to remove barriers of unnecessary qualifications. There is no need to require a bachelor's degree for a job that requires skills that are easy to learn and employer-specific processes to be followed" he explained.

A smile formed on Jim's face as he nodded in agreement. He was pleased to see that someone in the room was still actively listening and paying attention. "Yes, that's right," he said.

By the end of the meeting, Jim was as tired as a pastor after preaching an Easter sermon. He felt so many emotions running through his body and landed on gratitude as his dominant thought. As painful as this exchange was, he appreciated the opportunity to remove the need to give the "benefit of the doubt" that he and others had previously extended in the struggle for progress. He was also grateful for the clarity he needed to finalize his plan for the path forward in his organization. The truth had set him free.

8

BLACK AND WHITE TOGETHER

Jim drove home in silence. He needed time to listen in to his own thoughts but mostly the feelings in his body. His heart rate had returned to normal, but he knew that his heart would never really beat the same way again. He felt changed by the interaction at the CEO Consortium meeting. It was as if the innocence of white ignorance had been ripped away and David gave voice to the painful truth about why racial equity was so hard to solve for.

At the same time, he had an eternal optimism that things were in fact changing in America. Black and brown people had reached the emotional, financial, and political limit of the deference that holds systemic racism in place. He may not have had data but everything in his soul said that America's landscape around race was about to shift drastically. The next Black Lives Matter movement would not require empathy or fair-weather allies.

Jim was relieved to finally share his reorganization plan with senior leaders tomorrow. He began to reminisce about the first conversation he overheard that peaked his original interest in racial equity. In the years leading up to 2020, his unwavering commitment was the only thing that kept his organization on track. He knew that without making racial equity an entrenched part of their culture, his senior leadership team would have allowed old habits to set in and take them offtrack.

In the years since the pandemic, his planning for retirement had taken a back seat to the activation of his legacy plan. For the remaining twenty-four months until his last day, his goal was to demonstrate how organizations unravel from the years of discrimination that have crippled progress. The development and planning required in the past few months for the unveiling of his Equity and Impact Reorganization plan felt like keeping a heavy secret that was finally about to be released.

Jim stopped two streets from his last turn. He turned the car off and sat. He imagined Susan at the living room window waiting with some challenge from work that she wanted to talk through. He didn't have it in him tonight. He couldn't do another round of white fragility in his own home. He picked up his phone and dialed Roshunda one digit at a time.

9

WE WILL WALK
HAND IN HAND

ENGAGING IN ALLYSHIP

Jim was excited to introduce Juan Hernandez as a new member of his leadership team. In the years since Walter's departure from Jim's leadership team, it had become an established expectation that Jim had no tolerance for a substandard demonstration of leadership. Walter's strong vision of himself as the standard of success and his determination to hold the traditional power structure in place precluded him from making the personal adjustments required to lead in an inclusive environment. Jim was amazed at how the level of engagement and commitment of the remaining members of the leadership team had increased by that one departure.

Juan was the incoming Chief Operations Officer. He was a strategic hire who cost a pretty penny, but he had already recouped the recruiting fee and his signing bonus in process improvements and increased morale. In the final stages of the interviewing process, Jim was very honest with Juan about his goals around racial equity. Jim appreciated the perspective that Juan brought with his mixed heritage of a Mexican mother and Native American father who both made cultural heritage a priority in his home.

He understood the colorism and gender conversations as a light-skinned Hispanic man who has recognized some of the biases he was raised with. In the months since he had come on board, Jim and Juan developed a true friendship. Juan admitted that he often chose to benefit from being light skinned and pass as white. He knew that he had not fully reconciled the guilt of those choices, but often engaged in advocacy as an indirect attempt to ease his conscience.

Jim knew that there was the potential for some bad blood between Juan and the others who felt entitled to be considered as his successor as the thought of his retirement became more pronounced in his mind. Based on what he was seeing in this moment, privilege had worked to their disadvantage. Instead of having thirty real years of experience, many of them operated like mid-level managers with one year of experience that they were repeating over and over. Their arrogance about the value of their seniority combined with the narrow scope of their lived experience diminished their profiles when compared to some of the leaders below them who had overseas experience, blended families with various levels of diversity, and most importantly a genuine orientation toward inclusion. Jim had subtly been addressing the reality that as a group his legacy leaders were not adequately prepared for the volume of change in the workplace and the magnitude of personal development it required from them individually.

Jim planned to leverage Juan's commitment to building a strong culture and advocacy for inclusion. His hope was to expand and sustain the gains they had seen in the past few years since his original Aha moment in the restaurant, when he overheard a group of African American professionals discussing their experiences in the workplace.

As the executive conference room began to fill, Jasmine and Jim shared last-minute notes on today's agenda. It was Juan's first of the Senior Executive Leadership Focus (SELF) program session. Based on her one-on-one conversations with him, Jasmine was confident that he would be a great addition to the team. She was looking forward to all that he would bring to this allyship session.

After they had an appropriate opportunity to chat among themselves and top up their coffee, Jim launched the meeting. "Hey again everyone. I have really been looking forward to this session with Jasmine. Juan, you may remember me sharing some details about this program during your onboarding. Keeping our leadership chops sharp is one of our most important responsibilities in this company. So, we are engaged in a three-year program where we meet once per month or sometimes every six to eight weeks with Jasmine and her team to learn new leadership concepts. Sometimes it is actual training, sometimes she calls it group coaching where we discuss our key learnings from previous sessions and work through real situations occurring now. Jasmine, why don't you take it away and tell us what you have planned for today?"

Jim's tone and body language were all the introduction that Jasmine ever needed. His respect for her was evident and you could tell that he admired her ability to switch between facilitator, coach, and no-nonsense Black woman when necessary. She was not afraid of the stereotype, but rather used it strategically to her advantage.

"Welcome Juan and welcome back to everyone else. Let's start with a quick rewind from our last session on Leadership Agility. That session focused on our ability to demonstrate range in our responses. What stood out for you as key learnings?" Jasmine scanned the room and noticed a hand raised in the back. She nodded to give them permission to speak.

"The shift from Golden to Platinum Rule really had me thinking. It felt like that is the silver bullet I had been missing for a lot of this diversity and inclusion stuff. That one concept alone makes such a big difference. I think all leaders in our company need to get the training we are getting," he said.

"Thank you for sharing that. For those who may not remember, the Golden Rule says that we should treat people the way we want to be treated. However, the higher standard for inclusion is the Platinum Rule, which calls for us to treat people the way they want to be treated. Jasmine smiled as several leaders completed the sentence with her. Anyone else?" she asked. No one said anything more, so Jasmine switched to teacher mode. "OK, I will remind you of a few of the key points and you give me an example of how you applied it. Let's start with the first one—the ability to operate outside of personal preferences."

This time, another person from the front raised their hand to add to this point. "I have become more comfortable talking about race ever since that course a few months back. I realize that I always approached the experience from my preference of thinking everything is fair, everyone is equal, and especially that everyone is having the same experience as me. That analogy you made is so powerful. 'Talking to white people about race does sound like trying to explain the concept of wetness to a fish. We try to tell people there is no difference between wet and dry and then invite them to jump into the fishbowl to prove it.' That last part really got me. We can't tell them that there is no such thing as drowning. We sound ridiculous. That landed for me," she said enthusiastically.

Jasmine was pleased to hear how well the fish analogy stuck. She noticed that others in the room were growing more comfortable sharing so she moved along to the next point. "Next up, the ability to flex behavior based on the needs of others." Jasmine pointed to the next person eager to chime in.

"I had never attended the Pride Employee Resource Group events. I must admit that I was afraid because I am single, people might think that I am a member of that community. I realized that attending their events is not coming out. It is just an allyship behavior that shows solidarity. I participated in an icebreaker game and won one of those Silent Statement tumblers with the allyship checklist on it. I would have never imagined how much it means to people to see me using it."

"Yes," Jasmine began. "Just your behavior of showing up lets others know that you support them. Anyone else before we move on?" Jasmine skimmed the room once more and continued when she was certain no one else wanted to add their thoughts. "OK, the next point: capacity to deal with conflict," she said. This time, she didn't have to point to anyone. Someone jumped right on in.

"I had a few white people come to me complaining about their coworkers being excused to attend the listening sessions we held after the targeted shooting of Black people in Buffalo and the killing of Taiwanese people at the church. Normally, I probably would have agreed with them but the last training changed my perspective. I understand now why employees in those groups need time at work to process what has occurred. I understand why they probably don't need us there because we often focus on our need for comfort instead of their need for compassion in those moments. We need to stop this habit of constantly feeling left out and focus on other people's need to feel let in. So, I circled back with a few employees who I knew were emotionally impacted, asked them how they were doing and how I could support them best."

Jasmine was pleased with the depth of the sharing and felt ready to continue. "Those are all great examples, and they set the stage perfectly for today's session. It will be different from anything we have done before. I would like to introduce you to the concept of allyship through the Diversity Elements Solar System. First, I will explain the concept and then you are going to engage in several rounds of conversation to explore this approach for yourselves," Jasmine said as she turned to the projector that displayed her presentation. "First, I want to take you back for a moment to those middle school days when you got the solar system assignment. Remember having to go to the arts and crafts store to create a replica of the planets, followed by a class discussion?" Jasmine searched around the room for head nods and slight chuckles as everyone remembered having to do this annoying project at some point in their younger years. "Awesome! Now, I'm going to use that analogy to help you understand how each of those diversity elements lives in our heads and in our lives."

Jasmine moved forward throughout her explanation.

"Jupiter is the biggest planet in the Solar System and consider it to biggest diversity elements—the ones that are most impactful for you. For example, as an African American woman, race is my Jupiter. If I was white, it is possible that gender would be my Jupiter. Or if I was a nun, religion could have been my Jupiter." She continued after she saw a few head nods showing comprehension. "Do you remember Pluto? It is an interesting one because astronomers demoted Pluto to a dwarf planet as it is the smallest. It is also the farthest away from Earth in the Solar System. Pluto represents the diversity elements that are the least impactful for you. Least impactful meaning the ones that you don't think about. I must admit that as a cisgender heterosexual woman sexual orientation, gender identity, and expression live like Pluto for me. It is not something that I think about every day. This is where the core of most DEI conversations can go wrong. This is also why allyship is challenging for some people. If my Jupiter is your Pluto, how do I get you to care about my life experience? For example, if you are white, is it possible that race is your Pluto? So how do I get you to care about it as my most impactful element? What if national origin, such as being an American, is my Jupiter? Is it possible that anything I perceive as a treat to 'American culture' will be rejected and therefore inclusion behaviors become challenging?"

Jasmine got to her Partner Conversations slide and paused, then read the following on the slide: "Now, I would like for you all to find a partner and take five minutes to discuss:

1. Which diversity elements live like Jupiter for you? Biggest impact; always present and aware of at all times.
2. Which diversity elements live like Pluto for you? Least impact; you don't think about them.
3. What are the implications of your elements conflicting with other people's elements?

When the timer goes off, we will rotate and change partners."

Jasmine began to wander around the room, tuning in to bits and pieces of the conversations within the groups. These are the things she picked up on:

1. White male named Greg talks about his veteran status as his Jupiter diversity element. He realizes that when he sees someone kneel instead of standing for the flag it triggers a response of disrespect. The last session on Leadership Agility helped him understand that the act of kneeling was a passive and appropriate request for attention to the Black Lives Matter movement. After being ignored for so many years, he now understands that the frustration demonstrated in rioting really began by having the kneeling ignored.
2. A Black man named Dwayne on Jim's team who is normally very quiet realizes that his inability to embrace the LGBTQ community came from his fear that this community promotes the emasculation of Black men. Given that it is already difficult enough to manage the residual impact of being a Black man in America, this

normalization creates a concern for him raising his sons and mentoring young Black men. The session on Understanding Sexual Orientation, Gender Identity, and Expression (SOGIE) helped him to embrace the idea that this is not a learned behavior but rather an embodied element of our identity. He realized that it is hard enough for Black men to feel loved in this country. What we don't need is to make it even harder for them to find and enjoy it. This was the missing link he needed.

3. A white woman named Connie shares that she has begun to understand the tension between Black women and white women. Jasmine, sharing her experience that womanhood will never be as strong of an experience as Blackness, really shook her. Connie thought that all women were having the same experience. These trainings have helped her to see that her version of womanhood is significantly impacted by whiteness. That had never occurred to her before.

4. The only South Asian person on the team named Diya was actively engaged in the exercise and seemed delighted to finally be able to have language to explain how thinking and communication style were the most impactful diversity elements for her. Although everyone focused on her ethnicity as the most obvious identity, she felt that her personal history as an only child combined with the dominance of extroverts in almost every environment she ever worked in since college contributed to why she was not likely to share her views openly in meetings. Everyone assumed that she was a stereotypical quiet Asian woman when in fact she was simply wired for thoughtful introspection and had no need to struggle for airtime at work.

5. An African woman on the team named Thanda shared that religious beliefs was her Jupiter element and causes her to see all other aspects through this lens. Admittedly Christianity can be an exclusionary religion that does not have a natural respect for other expressions of faith. She originally resisted DEI training, including the training on race, because she felt like it was infringing on her religious beliefs that everyone is the same in God's eyes and she preferred to focus on our common membership in the human race rather than all of the elements that divide us. In addition, her experience fleeing a war-torn nation further reduces her tolerance for more conflict around race. In a previous session, Jasmine used Thanda's experience to note that everyone who experiences trauma has different coping mechanisms. Religion and avoiding differences are both logical coping mechanisms, based on Thanda's experience. Jasmine explained that she has chosen to focus some of her work on race as her personal coping mechanism for racial trauma. What's important is that everyone recognizes their approach as a coping mechanism while resisting the urge to see it as the only approach. That concept opened her up to becoming an ally for groups she never would have interacted with in the past.

Jasmine checked her watch and made the announcement that the final round of conversation was over. "Let's debrief your Aha moments from these conversations. Please use your app so we can see your thoughts on the screen. Plan to share your voiceover to help us understand the depth of your conversations," she said as she pointed to the screen.

1. We judge the need for allyship through our lens of how important the issue is to us; not how important it is to those in another group.

2. Allyship is difficult because we struggle to embrace what is important to other people.

3. How do we get people to care about diversity elements that don't live BIG for them?

4. I need to learn more about the allyship needs of other groups.

5. This exercise feels life changing in terms of how I now see the Black Lives Matter movement.

Jasmine purposefully allowed the group to type in their answers as an added anchoring of the learnings. Without saying a word, she looked around the room and invited them to practice the skill of talking about these topics.

Connie chimed in. "This exercise made me think about a term I have been hearing lately called 'empathy fatigue.' I didn't think much of it initially, but after this opportunity to share with others, it just occurred to me how difficult this must be to hear. How do you get tired of having empathy? Imagine how exhausting it must be still having to request empathy."

"That is a good notice of terminology you might want to be sensitive to."

Jasmine wrapped up her remarks with a serious tone. "Do not expect to be out in the world acting against allyship and have people think that you are a good person. It does not work that way. Help people in marginalized groups to feel like they are not alone by lending your voice and sometimes your privilege to their cause. Sometimes you must earn credit for being a good person."

The group took a welcomed break. Many sat still for several minutes before moving. Others turned to their neighbor and began chatting immediately. It was obvious that this session achieved the desired outcome and set the stage for the bombshell that was to come.

Jim waited for everyone to return and give him their attention naturally. Jasmine signaled that the next deck was ready before Jim launched the final segment of this day-long meeting. "Thanks Jasmine. I appreciated that last segment and everything it taught us about allyship. My hope is that you all have a new lens for how you see yourselves and my commitment for our leadership team to be a critical driver toward business results and corporate social responsibility." He looked at everyone individually as if to secure their commitment one more time.

Jim continued, "I also want to tee up where we are headed in the future. You will be expected to participate in an allyship immersion for the next ninety days. Your tasks are to:

1. immerse yourself in learning more about other groups, especially racial and ethnic experiences;
2. identify, build relationships with, and ultimately become a sponsor for two mid-level leaders;
3. attend and participate in three internal ERG events and one external community-based event each quarter."

"You will be reporting your allyship, sponsorship, and ERG activities into a confidential report compiled through this link on SharePoint. We will discuss and share our experiences and missteps as we learn together along the way. Your participation and key learnings from these exercises will be rolled up to my performance management notes on each of you, and used to create ratings and determine bonuses. Any questions about that first step?" Jim knew that was not the right way to phrase a leadership question as it closed the door on objections. However, he also knew that he was not willing to entertain objections in that moment. "After that, we will use the next ninety days to shift from allyship to activism. Allyship says that we are accepting the status quo. Activism says that we are here to change the status quo. And in many ways, it is going to take us—namely white men with power and influence—to repair the damage that white supremacy has caused. We are going to have to engage in activism willingly or activism will be enacted upon us. And if that happens, we probably won't like the results." Jim glanced around the room to confirm there were no further questions before moving on to his next point. "I saw this short video that sums up what needs to happen next. Caroline Wanga is President and CEO of Essence Ventures and she had this to say." Jim turned to his laptop, to pull up the video. He hit play, and Caroline Wanga's powerful baritone voice gripped the room.

"The future of activism is intrusive. It has no room for self-preservation. And it is measured by how the least of us are doing, not the best of us. So, no matter how successful I am, if the person next to me is not as successful, then I am not being the kind of activist I need to be. And I have to be prepared to give up some things so that others can have some things."[3]

Jim followed up with further comments. "The most impactful of all the strategies we will undertake this year is the Equity and Impact Reorganization. In lieu of layoffs, we will be assessing performance ratings for everyone in the company. We will keep only the most productive employees who demonstrate our values and the corporate culture around engagement, inclusion, and innovation that we have been attempting to build for the last several years. Then each team's salary will be put into a pool and rebalanced to be equitably distrib-

---

3   https://publish.twitter.com/?query=https%3A%2F%2Ftwitter.com%2FGlblCtzn%2F status%2F1653178857480912897andwidget=Tweet.

uted. Effective leaders who make the cut will receive a standard percentage above their team's salaries. Employees will be assessed based on education and experience and we will make adjustments where legacy inequalities and comparable experiences fill the gap. This will become a model for how equity is demonstrated in an organization," he said. Jim could sense some reluctance in the room. Discussing pay openly brought about discomfort. He knew he would have to offer some reassurance that he too would be impacted by this change. "And just so you know, my salary will be put into the pool, and I fully expect that it will be reduced in service of the overall leadership percentage formula. What questions do you have about this initiative?" Jim changed his voice and demeanor to genuinely invite questions and conversation.

Everyone looked at each other waiting for an unidentified brave soul to speak first. Greg asked, "Has the Board approved this?"

"Great question, Greg," Jim replied. "They have. I presented why this was a better approach than the standard 'cut and slash' layoffs that we have seen. I truly believe that by cutting the dead weight out of the organization and being intentional about a radical move toward equity, we will increase employee engagement, a true experience of inclusion and belonging, spark innovation, and even increase retention over time. Turnover costs are killing us right now and it is from good people leaving asshole managers. Our projections indicate that even if I am wrong about increased productivity and reduced turnover, we will save so much just from what the dead weight is costing us in discretionary effort, lawsuits, and bad publicity."

Diya raised her hand to add her thoughts. "This approach isn't really new. Companies around the world have been using it for decades. It really does work."

Jim jumped in as if he just remembered something. "Thanks, Diya, for mentioning that. It reminds me to talk about another critical element. I am prepared for those who will criticize this as a socialist/ communist leaning activity. I can't control the irrational fears and political ideology of others, but I do have a specific spreadsheet that explains this as a business strategy that speaks to the bottom line. What people don't realize is that when they deny the financial merits of this strategy in favor of political rhetoric, they are showing everyone that the real agenda is for the richest 5 percent to maintain economic power over the remaining 95 percent. My plan shows how we ensure that shareholders will continue to make a significant return on their investment while we make a significant impact on our community. There is no layoff plan that could yield as much as this strategy will yield over the next five years. We need to address the actual problems in our organization and stop ignoring that impact of strong leadership. Our employees proved during COVID that they will put the organization on their backs and carry us over the finish line. It is now time to demonstrate the same level of commitment to them."

It was clear that everyone was not totally sold on Jim's radical sounding plan. Most of the apprehension in the room was a combination of lack of clarity about the details of how to execute it and the potential negative impact on each of them individually. In essence, Jim's plan was to clear the deck, reshuffle it, and deal everyone a new hand. It was the next level marriage of business strategy and equity that screamed "We are onboard for real solutions that make sense to adjust for the past and make an impact for the future. Someday had finally arrived and it was today."

10

THE LORD WILL SEE US THROUGH

SOLUTION SPACE

Jasmine was feeling the emotional effect of that weird period between Juneteenth and the Fourth of July. As a general rule, she never referred to the holiday as Independence Day. It was a deliberate and intentional act of disrespect. She felt it was now clear that the Declaration of Independence was not designed for everyone and may never be applied to everyone. It was particularly painful to have the Supreme Court abolish affirmative action just before America launched its annual patriotic masturbation with picnics and parades.

Jasmine took Friday to grieve and allow herself the benefits of feeling the disappointment, disgust, and anger of the SCOTUS decision. She recorded a short video for her clients and the genuine allies, who she knew were personally struggling with the decision while being asked to craft empty statements in response. She specifically wore her red "No Racism Formed Against Me Shall Prosper" T-shirt and pressed record before she got out of the car. "Hi everyone. I'm recording this video, basically as a virtual hug. Maybe, it's the hug I need myself. But I'm kind of thinking that you are feeling somewhat like me today—where this is a difficult day to be us. I really just wanted to send you some encouragement and acknowledge how today feels, and hopefully renew and inspire you." Jasmine paused and repositioned herself allowing viewers to read across her breasts.

"There aren't many professions where you feel like society doesn't want you to succeed. I just want to remind you that they want us to quit. They want us to give up. I know for me, that makes me want to do this even more. But it also makes it OK to just acknowledge that this is hard. I don't really have any answers, at least not right now. When I have a few more things figured out I will let you all know. For now, I'm just remembering what my Mama used to say...'*there's more than one way to skin a cat*,' and strategy is still a thing. There are ways we can operate inside our organizations in spite of all this. So, that's it. Be well until it is well." Jasmine ended her recording and posted it to her social media platforms. The heart emoji replies and encouraging messages were comforting, but she could still not help feeling sad.

By Saturday morning, she had moved beyond the emotions, put her thinking cap on, and came up with a few next steps to address the key issues behind the dismantling of affirmative action.

1. College administrators should begin a communication campaign to remind people of the behavior that led to the implementation of affirmative action (i.e., race was used as a disqualifying factor for admission) and what steps will be taken going forward.

2. Affirmative action was implemented as a necessary measure to override the legacy bias of systemic racism and discrimination in admissions. So, we have already proven that we cannot be trusted with objective decision-making in this area.

3. Alumni of color should halt all donations to institutions if they cannot be allocated as the donor dictates and until a documented plan is in place to ensure how bias will be

mitigated in the admission process. Authentic allies may join this campaign.

4. Chief Admissions Officers should outline how the admissions process will change and put systems in place to monitor how biases will be eliminated in the admissions process going forward.

5. University senior leadership should consider how benefit is offered in areas beyond race and ethnicity, for example, legacy admissions should no longer be allowed or promoted.

6. Trustee Boards should consider how the practice of faculty tenure creates an unfair advantage to those applying now and if the perpetuation of this practice is serving students appropriately in a dynamic world where information and solutions need to be more agile than ever.

Whether or not her clients used these ideas, Jasmine knew that each one of them had the potential to create exponential impact when combined with a sincere commitment to academic principles of diversity of thought and scholarship in integrity.

———————

It was the first time the Happy Hour Posse had been to this restaurant. All they knew was that it was Black-owned with five stars and a slew of positive reviews. Eli was the first to arrive as usual, and their tardiness gave him some necessary time to reflect.

His life had come full circle. He remembered the other roundtable discussions and how he often felt tense in the presence of his friends. But now he was feeling fulfilled in his career and accomplished as a father, whose young adult daughter was beginning to build a relationship with his significant other. He was happy about the relationship his friends now had with Nathan, and how good it felt to finally be his authentic self. He was pleased that Roshunda and Maya felt comfortable enough to ask Nathan tough questions. And he was even more proud of how Nathan handled the responses with the credibility of a professor and the care of a big cousin. Life would continue 'life-ing,' but it made such a difference to know that he had a loving partner by his side and out in the world.

Shane and LaToya arrived next, looking more in love than ever. As soon as LaToya sat down, Eli couldn't help but notice the extravagant bling on her left ring finger. "Y'all getting married!" Eli shouted in his family reunion voice.

Shane and LaToya grinned at each other, blushing with excitement. Shane placed a finger to his mouth in an attempt to calm Eli, "Yeah man. She said yes." Shane turned to his new fiancé and gave her a heart melting gaze that screamed "provision and protection." LaToya responded by tilting her head to his shoulder in a gesture that said, "worthy of my submission."

Maya eased in quietly and sat next to Eli. "What are you two over there grinning about?" she said in the Caribbean accent she thought she hid. LaToya slowly started to flash and wiggle her ring finger allowing the diamond to speak for itself. "Whew chile!" Maya said. "This brother loves you honey! This ring is designed to repel anyone who might be looking your way. I love it! Just love it! Congratulations!"

Maya sounded so sincere in her congratulations that it caused LaToya to have a rare moment of wondering about Maya's love life. Everyone knew that she had been divorced a long time ago but she didn't ever talk about having a significant other. LaToya made a mental note to schedule time with her to get some Auntie wisdom that would help start her married life off on the right foot.

Roshunda arrived fashionably late looking like a hot mess. She seemed rushed and unsettled, the complete opposite of her normally tailored and chic self. She sat down shyly and tried to raise her energy level to greet everyone. The first topic of conversation was clearly LaToya's ring. Roshunda struggled to muster the energy to offer genuine excitement. In fact, she chose to bypass it passively by saying, "Oh Black Love. I love it!" No one could deny the beauty of her blessing but only those who knew the backstory heard the subtle shade that she was throwing as well.

Shane wasn't about to let anything ruin this moment for him and LaToya. He raised his glass and used his commanding voice to get everyone's attention. "Let me propose a toast. To my beautiful future wife, and our friends at this table. I appreciate you guys so much for all you have taught me on the journey to becoming the world's best husband and one day the world's best father. My intention is to strengthen our community starting with my household." Their glasses clinked as they summoned the Holy Spirit to bless this union forever.

After the meal, Maya took the conversation in a new direction. "I honestly believe that the only way we will rebuild our communities is if we take our power back and engage in new behaviors. We need a new approach." Everyone nodded in agreement. Maya felt like there was real potential in her comment and continued. "I am sure that each of us can come up with two or three things that we will do differently to move the needle on racial equity. I will start." Maya shifted in her seat so that she could see all of them. "One, mentor more young people—to whatever extent those 'know it alls' will listen to grown folks." She looked at Roshunda, laughed, and gave her a hug. Roshunda rolled her eyes and hugged her back.

"I'm sorry I didn't mean to say that part out loud," Maya said with a hand over her mouth. "I must admit that I am warming up to the idea that millennials and Gen Z folks may be interested in hearing what we have to say if we demonstrate a willingness to meet them halfway and communicate in a way that helps them listen. I am going to do better with that." She saw Roshunda giving her a side eye when she paused to take another sip of her wine. "OK, second, I am going to be more intentional and patient with the differences that exist between our people. We have been so oppressed for so long that we have lost the ability to appreciate the many ways that we are different. I have learned so much about gender identity and expression. I must admit that education reduces resistance and promotes acceptance."

Everyone nodded in agreement. "And lastly, I will continue to promote the talent in our community. Whenever possible, I look for talented people of color to work with my company. Not only to support their businesses but also to showcase them to my clients. Every time they show up with their awesome selves, it provides examples of the pipeline white people keep saying they can't find. My hope is that those interactions rest in their subconscious and get resurrected the next time they find themselves in an interview with a person of color. We don't have a pipeline problem. We have a perspective problem. Maybe seeing themselves up on the walls everywhere contributes to some white people to continuing to see themselves as the 'best candidate' and ignore contrary evidence of others' performance in their roles," Maya finished her speech with an excited nod.

Everyone raised a glass to give a cheer to the points Maya made. "OK, I'll go next," Roshunda said. "I am going to be more deliberate about flipping the script in HR. Teach people how to one … not share salary history in an interview. That question is currently illegal[4] in a number of states including California, Georgia, North Carolina, and good ole' DC. But we all need to agree to never answer it in any interview. Second, negotiate other elements of a role, and not just salary. Remote and hybrid work, vacation time, signing, moving, and

---

4   https://www.paycor.com/resource-center/articles/states-with-salary-history-bans/.

retention bonuses. We need to conduct reverse interviews. Meaning, learn to interview companies about the execution of the DEI website narrative, tangible outcomes, and organizational culture.

"At our company, I am going to hold hiring managers account-able for the choices they don't make. I'm going to ask them pointed questions to justify decisions that support the status quo. Like, what elements of the diverse candidate's experience were not a fit for the role? Then listen for them to automatically switch to what they preferred about the majority candidate. At that point, it is my job to challenge them to stay in the question that I asked."

"Ever since I transitioned into HR, I feel like we have abdicated our power in that struggle to get a seat at the table. Sometimes it feels like they gave us a stool and we accept being the least of the apostles. No other discipline allows line managers to jeopardize the area that they have responsibility for. But somehow HR has allowed hiring managers to put the company at risk under the guise of being a business partner," Roshunda took a breath and concluded. "Our CEO just unveiled an Equity and Impact Reorganization plan that has the potential to change the game if it is executed properly."

"OK, OK," Eli began. "I'm going to change my language. I rebuke the vocabulary and emotion of 'imposter syndrome.' We, the ones who have to be over-qualified for most opportunities, are not imposters." The gang all gave a round of yeses in agreement. "The ones who get roles based on an inflation of their potential or the benefit of sameness with the decision-maker are imposters. I will no longer carry the 'less than enough' weight of that label. Now I correct people when they say 'slave trade' because that implies an equal exchange of value. It was human trafficking. Since we have been oriented to that term in recent years, I am going to start calling it the 'human traf-ficking of African people.' I am also going to stop talking about the 'browning of America,' because that is what is making racists nervous and trigger-happy. If we were smart, we would never have advertised that and just let them wake up one morning in 2045, look around, and figure out that they are outnumbered."

"And I'm not going to say 'minorities' anymore either. I will qualify when I am talking about the 'corporate majority' or the 'corporate minority.' The term will change depending on what conversation I am sitting in."

Everyone turned their attention to LaToya waiting for her to chime in. "Well, that's a lot to follow. Let's see," LaToya paused to think deeply about what she wanted to say. She fidgeted with her new engagement ring as she gathered her thoughts. "I'm gonna be intentional about my coping strategies. We need to rethink the concept of 'excellence' in favor of adding 'extra' value. We have allowed this work culture to condition us to operate at a higher level than others at all times. Meanwhile, white people get credit for potential they have yet to demonstrate, applauded for their efforts, and overall flourish in their mediocrity. I am going to start treating my discretionary effort like a business asset—you will get the amount that you have paid for. And since my personal best is better than most, I can still be a top performer for the sixty-eight cents on the dollar that you are paying me now. And then, I am going to take the rest of my discretionary effort and emotional energy and start a business off the side of my kitchen table. One day I will be like Maya and work from the Caribbean whenever I grow weary of Amerikkka. Second, I'm going to make time for emotional self-care. I am going to give myself 'white woman' days." Everyone looked at LaToya like an alien had taken over her body. She chuckled at their looks of confusion. "What I mean is, there are times when I make a deliberate attempt to walk through the world like a white woman. Make my thoughts and feelings the center of my perspective and response. It takes a lot of energy to always be concerned about how things look and sound to others. I am going to release that sometimes. And guess what else, if you interpret me as angry—I will make that response your choice and totally disassociate it from my concern. I am going to take on damsel in distress energy, hang up my superwoman cape, and let the Universe support my needs. I can do most things independently, but I will opt not to, and wait for someone to help me. I'm gonna take my time crossing the street and force each motorist to wait rather than running to get out of their way," LaToya added with a big grin on her face.

"Well said, Babe," Shane added. "I guess it's my turn. I'm going to use my voice strategically. Speak up in meetings, sometimes with questions like, 'Can you please help me understand how you came to that position?' Or 'Does that position align with the data available?' Or 'How might that sound from the other perspective?'"

He continued, "Sometimes with statements like, 'I am not clear on how that aligns with the DEI goals we expressed,' 'Guess what else? I am gonna keep my folding chair handy, at work and always.'" They all broke out laughing at the reference to the Montgomery Brawl. Everyone knew that had become the new battle cry for Fuck Around and Find Out because that was—the day.

Shane took a brief glance at everyone as they finished their meals and sipped their wine. It forced him to think deeper. He enjoyed their talks, but he really wanted to know what was next.

"This is a great conversation for us to be having. But who is having this conversation with white people? Where do they go to learn how to be better allies? They are already having empathy fatigue only a few years after George Floyd's killing supposedly woke them up. It was painful to hear them say 'I didn't know' in the summer of 2020. And I want to scream every time someone criticizes the lack of progress with DEI a few years later. And now we have to listen to them saying that they don't want to be woke," Shane said.

Roshunda chimed in, attempting to redirect everyone to the bright side. "We have made some progress with the Crown Act being passed in a few states."

Maya interjected, "I don't want to hear about the Crown Act unless I'm suing someone for violating it. I am offended by the notion we need legislation to police our hair. What I know for sure is that if white peoples' hair defied gravity like ours does, any style that dropped straight toward your shoulders would be considered unprofessional. Do you realize that almost every style we create is designed to manage gravity not our hair? Enough with that bullshit. Ain't nobody got time for that. I suggest that we stop acknowledging it with debate."

"We need to refresh ourselves on what the old school leaders used to teach. When I went to Egypt on an educational tour with Dr. Yosef Ben-Jochannan in 1991, it was life changing to have him and his protégés teach us about the pyramids and mostly about ourselves. Dr. Frances Cress Welsing was a renowned Black psychiatrist. I did marriage counseling with her. She was amazing. Everyone needs to read her books and listen to her lectures. There is so much wisdom there. I found this classic video of Dr. John Henrik Clarke. He and Dr. Ben were buddies. In fact, y'all need to see this video clip of him breaking it down on what needs to happen next for Black people." Maya paused to pull out her phone and find the video. She laid her phone on the center of the table so the group could hear:

"We cannot ask the people who programmed us into oblivion to program us out of it. Education has but one honorable purpose. One alone. Everything else is nonsense. That is to train the student to be a respectful and a responsible handler of power. People do not train you on how to take their power

away from them when they hold power by controlling you. To expect this of other people is a contradiction in terms. Freedom is something you do not wish upon; you do not dream upon. Freedom is something you take with your own hands."[5]

Everyone sat in silence for a moment and seemed to be in sync with the magnitude of personal and professional changes that they had all been through. These conclusions and new ways of being were the cumulative effect of working while Black, surviving a pandemic, and the trauma of watching the rise and fall of white allies for and against racial equity. Intellectually they wished that they could unpack these changes and put them into a neat box to explain all of the ways they had changed and been changed. But there is no such algorithm. It was like a meeting notification that popped up in the collective subconscious as a reminder of what was no longer acceptable.

Someday is today.

---

5   https://www.youtube.com/watch?v=Iadan9RnEIo.

ABOUT THE AUTHOR

Allison Manswell is a seasoned talent management executive with over twenty-five years of proven experience in human resources, organizational effectiveness, employee and leadership development, diversity and inclusion interventions with Fortune-ranked companies, mid-size organizations and boutique consulting firms. She is author of *Listen In: Crucial Conversations on Race in the Workplace* and the sequel *Someday is Today: Achieving Racial Equity in the Workplace.*

She holds the industry credential of Certified Professional in Talent Development (CPTD) from the Association for Talent Development. In addition, Ms. Manswell holds an MBA in Leadership and has been an on-ground and online faculty member for undergraduate and graduate programs. Her career began with a bachelor's degree in justice and law enforcement and roles with the Royal Canadian Mounted Police and Revenue Canada.

Ms. Manswell is the founder and CEO of Path Forward Consulting, a boutique firm that leverages her expertise in:

- consulting with small, mid-size and large-scale organizations including assessments and culture shift
- training from design through delivery and evaluation; and
- coaching from individual contributors to senior executives and groups

She has grown the firm from a small start-up to a globally recognized industry leader recognized as:

- Top 10 Leadership Development Firm by *HR Tech Outlook Magazine*
- Top 10 Diversity & Inclusion Firm by *HR Tech Outlook Magazine*
- Top 10 Organizational Effectiveness Firm by *Manage HR Magazine*
- Most Influential Race Specialist (USA) by *Acquisitions International Magazine*
- 50 Most Innovative Companies to Watch by *CIO Bulletin*
- 50 Innovators of the Year by *CIO Bulletin*

As a recognized subject matter expert, her media appearances include NBC, NPR, and many contributions to professional conferences. Ms. Manswell is also a sought-after speaker who has worked internationally in the US, Canada, the Caribbean, and Brazil.

Mostly importantly, she is the mother of three sons, who have grown from being her millennial roommates to accomplished young men who are all scholars/athletes/entrepreneurs. Her hobbies include astrology and traveling for family and cultural events where food, music, and dancing are involved.

For more information or to book Allison Manswell,
visit AllisonManswell.com.

www.ingramcontent.com/pod-product-compliance
Lightning Source LLC
Chambersburg PA
CBHW051723260326
41914CB00031B/1700/J